# Part 1:
## K–2 Reading Foundational Skills Screeners

# Part 2:
## K–6 Foundational Skills Quick Checks

# Table of Contents

The *Benchmark Advance* literacy program has ten units per grade in Grades K–6. Each three-week unit focuses on a particular topic that is developed through literary, informational texts, and/or opinion/argument pieces. Instruction in each unit focuses on reading, vocabulary, language acquisition, word study, and writing. In grades K–2, instruction also emphasizes foundational literacy skills.

It is important to establish students' levels and literacy skills. This book provides test screeners and foundational skills quick checks designed to help teachers make decisions about placement and instructional planning for students in the *Benchmark Advance* literacy program.

Part 1 includes the Reading Foundational Skills Screener Tests for Levels A–C, which correspond to Kindergarten, Grade 1, and Grade 2. These assessments are intended to help establish a baseline for each student, from which you may monitor each student's progress through the school year.

Part 2 includes the Reading Foundational Skills Quick Checks, which enable teachers to track students as they progress and determine if they are learning the skills they need to move to the next level. Specific assessments also help educators identify students' weaknessess or areas in which each student may require additional instruction or reinforcement.

In addition, you may use the Foundational Skills Quick Checks to evaluate new, transfering students, and English learners' literacy placement during the school year. For example, if a student enters your class in October, you may want to administer a one-minute fluency quick check at the student's grade level to determine the student's reading development.

## Introduction

The Reading Foundational Skills Screener Test has three levels, A, B, and C. These levels correspond to Kindergarten, Grade 1, and Grade 2. Test content is based on the Reading Foundational Skills taught at each level in *Benchmark Advance*.

The screener tests should be administered at the beginning of the school year to establish a baseline for each student and to help determine their instructional literacy needs. Students may take each level test screener that seems appropriate. For example, for transfer students or English learners, you may want to begin the test at Level A and continue until you determine the appropriate setting placement for each student.

The screener tests are designed to be administered in a small-group setting. However, if some or all of your students are not able to take the test, you may want to administer it one-on-one, in a secluded setting, instead. Students may develop reading foundational skills at very different rates. The purpose of the screener tests is to collect helpful information about their literacy needs. If a student has difficulty or shows frustration in answering questions, you can stop the administration of the test and try again at another time.

The chart below shows the content of the test and the numbers of questions, or items, at each level. Estimated times for administering the test are provided at the beginning of the directions for each level screener. There are also directions for how to administer and score each level of the test. You will find recommended instructional materials for students to differentiate your instruction to meet all students' needs. You can use the foundational skills quick checks in Part 2 and the chart on page 8 to determine specific Intervention lessons for students' needs.

| Level A | Items | Level B | Items | Level C | Items |
|---------|-------|---------|-------|---------|-------|
| Letter Recognition | 5 | Letter Recognition | 5 | Consonants | 10 |
| Phonological Awareness | 5 | Letter Sounds | 5 | Vowels | 10 |
| Letter Sounds | 5 | Consonants | 5 | Word Recognition | 5 |
| Word Recognition | 5 | Vowel Sounds | 5 | Word Study Skills | 5 |
| | | Word Recognition | 5 | | |
| Total | 20 | | 25 | | 30 |

## Administering the Test

When you are ready to administer the test, we suggest that you read through and become familiar with the the level you intend to administer. Then, for each student who will take the test, make a copy of the relevant student pages. Have each student write his or her name on the test pages before starting the test; or, if students are unable to do this, write their names in for them. Read the directions aloud to the students taking the test, have them mark their answers on the student pages, and then collect the pages for scoring.

Each level screener has four or five parts and is generally designed to be administered in consecutive order in two sittings. However, the test is flexible. You may decide to give the test one part at a time—and only the parts you consider appropriate at a given time or for particular students—or you may give the parts in any sequence.

The directions in bold type are intended to be read aloud. Text in regular type is for your information and should not be read aloud. Each part of the test begins with a sample question. If needed, you may show students how to mark their answers with the sample. It will not be scored.

To begin, read the directions. Then, read each question aloud. Pause after each question to allow time for students to mark their answers.

## Scoring the Test

After administering the test, use the Answer Key for each level to score each student's test. The Answer Key indicates the correct answer for each question.

You will find Scoring Charts for each level screener as well. To use the Scoring Charts, make a copy for each student who takes the test. Circle the question number for each question answered correctly and cross out the number of each question answered incorrectly.

Count the number of questions answered correctly. Mark the number in the appropriate box on the Scoring Chart. Refer to the Percentage Chart for Part of Test and Total Test to find the percentage scores.

# Intepreting Test Scores

A student's score will help you determine his or her instructional placement. You will need to consider a student's score on each subtest and on the total test. The subtest scores can help you identify instructional needs.

In general, a student who scores **90% or above** on the total test has scored above grade level. The student will need to be challenged during instruction, OR you may want to administer the next test to see how the student scores.

> **For instructional planning,** refer to "Meeting the Needs of Students Who Are Advanced Learners" in the K–2 Additional Resources in *Benchmark Advance.*

A student who scores from **60 to 89%** on the total test has scored at about grade level and may enter the instructional program for Level A at Kindergarten, Unit 1; for Level B at Grade 1, Unit 1; and for Level C at Grade 2, Unit 1.

> **For instructional planning,** refer to foundational lessons in *Benchmark Advance,* which can be found in the phonics and shared reading mini-lessons as well as in the *Reader's Theater Handbook.*

A student who scores below **60%** on the total test has scored below grade level and will likely need extra attention and intervention in the instructional program at that level.

> **For instructional planning,** refer to the correct grade level of *Benchmark Advance Intervention* phonics and word recognition lessons. For Level A refer to Grade K, for Level B refer to Grade 1, and for Level C refer to Grade 2.

If a student's test score does not clearly indicate an appropriate placement, then we recommend administering additional assessments. Depending on the student's situation, you may want to use the foundational skills quick checks in Part 2 to collect more information and determine further instructional need.

## Introduction

The purpose of this component is to help assess a student's development of foundational skills in Grades K–6. Foundational Skills Quick Checks are organized in the following categories:

**Print Concepts**

**Phonological Awareness**

**Phonics and Word Recognition**

**Fluency**

All of the quick checks are aligned with the reading foundational skills taught in each unit and each level of the *Benchmark Advance* literacy program, Grades K–6.

These quick checks are designed to be short, quick assessments of specific skills. You may administer a quick check to one or more students and record the results. Information drawn from these can be used to help plan or refine instruction for students based on individual and very specific needs.

Many of the quick checks are designed to be used in pretesting and posttesting, before and after instruction, and to determine how much progress students have made. The information from these may be used for periodic assessment of students' reading foundational skills in K–6, to monitor students' progress, to identify specific instructional needs, and/or to adjust student placement in the program.

In most cases, these quick checks are intended for individual use, to be administered one-on-one, although some are suitable for small groups. Directions for administering and scoring the quick checks are provided in each section.

## Description of the Quick Check Bank

The Reading Foundational Skills Quick Checks are organized by reading level and by foundational skill. Quick checks that assess the most basic skills and understanding, such as print concepts and letter recognition, appear at the beginning of the quick check bank. More advanced skills, such as recognizing variant vowels and words with prefixes, appear later. For some skills that are taught in Grades 1–5, such as syllable patterns, the quick checks are ordered by difficulty level from easy to hard. For example, the first syllable pattern quick check is based on syllable patterns taught in Grade 1, and the later quick checks are based on syllable patterns taught in Grade 5.

However, the quick check bank is not intended to be used in sequential order from beginning to end. You may dip into the bank at any stage to assess any of the skills or concepts being taught in the literacy program.

## Suggestions for Using the Bank

The table of contents for the quick check bank lists all of the skills taught and assessed in the program. You may assess any of the skills listed by going to that section of the bank, reviewing the materials available, and choosing the one(s) you wish to use.

In general, within each section, you will find the teacher materials first. If there are separate student pages, those appear after the teacher directions in each section. In most cases, you will need to read aloud from the teacher pages and record the results of each quick check on a teacher page. Make one copy of the teacher page(s) you need for each student you plan to assess. If there is a student page that students will need to look at and/or mark, then make one copy of the student page(s) for each student.

At the beginning of the school year, you may plan to administer either the Reading Foundational Skills Screener (Grades K–2). Based on Screener results and classroom observation, adminster the quick checks as needed during the year to help you make instructional decisions and/or match students to appropriate Intervention lessons. Results of these assessments can help you select appropriate Intervention lessons for each student by using the table on page 8.

# Intervention Lessons Aligned to the Foundational Skills

| Foundational Skills | Grade K Intervention | Grade 1 Intervention | Grade 2 Intervention | Grade 3 Intervention |
|---|---|---|---|---|
| **Phonological and Phonemic Awareness (PA)** | | | | |
| Word Awareness | PA, Lessons 4, 5 | PA, Lessons 11, 12 | PA, Lessons 11, 12 | PA, Lesson 11 |
| Syllable Awareness | PA, Lessons 4, 5 | PA, Lessons 11, 12 | PA, Lessons 11, 12 | PA, Lessons 1–4 |
| Listening for Rhyme | PA, Lesson 1 | PA, Lesson 8 | PA, Lesson 8 | PA, Lesson 9 |
| Identifying Rhyme | PA, Lessons 1, 2 | PA, Lessons 8, 9 | PA, Lessons 8, 9 | PA, Lessons 9, 15, 17 |
| Producing Rhyme | PA, Lessons 1, 2, 3 | PA, Lessons 8, 9, 10 | PA, Lessons 8, 9, 10 | PA, Lesson 10 |
| Listening for Initial Sounds | PA, Lessons 6, 7, 10, 11 | PA, Lessons 6, 13, 14, 17 | PA, Lessons 6, 13, 14, 17 | PA, Lessons 6, 7, 16, 17 |
| Listening for Final Sounds | PA, Lessons 8, 10, 11 | PA, Lessons 6, 15, 16, 17 | PA, Lessons 6, 15, 16, 17 | PA, Lessons 6, 7, 16, 17 |
| Listening for Medial Sounds | PA, Lessons 10, 11 | PA, Lessons 2, 4, 6, 16, 17 | PA, Lessons 2, 4, 6, 16, 17 | PA, Lessons 6, 7, 16, 17 |
| Differentiating Initial Sounds | PA, Lessons 3, 7, 13 | PA, Lessons 3, 10, 14, 19 | PA, Lessons 3, 10, 14, 19 | PA, Lessons 6, 7, 16, 17 |
| Differentiating Final Sounds | PA, Lesson 8 | PA, Lesson 15 | PA, Lesson 15 | PA, Lessons 6, 7, 16, 17 |
| Differentiating Medial Sounds | PA, Lesson 11 | PA, Lesson 17 | PA, Lesson 17 | PA, Lessons 6, 7, 16, 17 |
| Differentiating Initial, Medial, and Final Sounds | PA, Lesson 10 | PA, Lesson 16 | PA, Lesson 16 | PA, Lessons 6, 7, 16, 17 |
| Blending Onset and Rime | PA, Lesson 8 | PA, Lesson 15 | PA, Lesson 15 | PA Lesson 14 |
| Segmenting Onset and Rime | PA, Lesson 8 | PA, Lesson 15 | PA, Lesson 15 | PA, Lesson 14 |
| Segmenting Phonemes | PA, Lesson 10 | PA, Lessons 6, 7, 16 | PA, Lessons 6, 7, 16 | PA, Lesson 16 |
| Blending Phonemes | PA, Lesson 14 | PA, Lessons 5, 20 | PA, Lessons 5, 20 | PA, Lessons 5, 11 |
| Substituting Initial Sounds | PA, Lesson 13 | PA, Lesson 19 | PA, Lesson 19 | PA, Lesson 19 |
| Substituting Medial Sounds | PA, Lesson 13 | PA, Lesson 19 | PA, Lesson 19 | PA, Lesson 19 |
| Substituting Final Sounds | PA, Lesson 13 | PA, Lesson 19 | PA, Lesson 19 | PA, Lesson 19 |
| Substituting Sounds (initial, medial, final) | PA, Lesson 13 | PA, Lesson 19 | PA, Lesson 19 | PA, Lesson 19 |

| Foundational Skills | Grade K Intervention | Grade 1 Intervention | Grade 2 Intervention | Grade 3 Intervention |
|---|---|---|---|---|
| **Print Concepts (PC)** | | | | |
| Book Awareness | PC, Lesson 1 | PC, Lesson 3 | PC, Lesson 3 | PC, Lesson 3 |
| Picture/Word Differentiation | PC, Lesson 2 | PC, Lesson 4 | PC, Lesson 4 | PC, Lesson 4 |
| Letter Concept | PC, Lesson 3 | PC, Lesson 5 | PC, Lesson 5 | PC, Lesson 5 |
| Word Concept | PC, Lesson 4 | PC, Lesson 6 | PC, Lesson 6 | PC, Lesson 6 |
| Spoken Word/Written Word Connection | PC, Lessons 5, 6 | PC, Lessons 7, 8 | PC, Lessons 7, 8 | PC, Lesson 7 |
| Uppercase and Lowercase Letters | PC, Lesson 7 | PC, Lesson 9 | PC, Lesson 9 | PC, Lesson 9 |
| Letter/Number Identification | PC, Lesson 8 | PC, Lesson 10 | PC, Lesson 10 | PC, Lesson 10 |
| Features of a Sentence | PC, Lesson 1 | PC, Lesson 1 | PC, Lesson 1 | PC, Lesson 1 |
| Punctuation | PC, Lesson 1 | PC, Lesson 2 | PC, Lesson 2 | PC, Lesson 2 |
| **Phonics and Word Recognition (PWR)** | | | | |
| Consonant Letter Recognition | PWR, Lessons 1–28, PC, Lesson 7 | N/A | N/A | N/A |
| Vowel Letter Recognition | PWR, Lessons 29–35; PC, Lesson 7 | N/A | N/A | N/A |
| Consonant Sounds | PWR, Lessons 1–28 | PWR, Lessons 1, 11, 41–72 | PWR, Lessons 53, 76–103 | N/A |
| Consonant Blends | N/A | PWR, Lessons 2–4, 10 | PWR, Lessons 42–44 | PWR, Lessons 40–44 |
| Consonant Clusters | N/A | PWR, Lesson 5 | PWR, Lesson 45 | PWR, Lesson 44 |
| Consonant Digraphs | N/A | PWR, Lessons 6–8 | PWR, Lessons 46–48 | PWR, Lessons 45–47 |
| Short Vowels | PWR, Lessons 29–38, 44–47 | PA, Lessons 1, 2 PWR, Lessons 69–78, 84–87 | PA, Lessons 1, 2 PWR, Lessons 104–113, 119–122 | N/A |
| Long Vowels | PWR, Lessons 39–43, 44–47 | PA, Lessons 1, 3, 4 PWR, Lessons 12–16, 79–83, 84–87 | PA, Lessons 1, 3, 4 PWR, Lessons 3–5, 7, 8, 15, 54–63 | N/A |
| r-Controlled Vowels | N/A | PWR, Lessons 22–24 | PWR, Lessons 13–14 | N/A |
| Variant Vowels | N/A | PWR, Lessons 22–24 | PWR, Lessons 3–5, 7, 8, 65–67 | PWR, Lessons 6, 7, 15 |

# Intervention Lessons Aligned to the Foundational Skills (continued)

| Foundational Skills | Grade K Intervention | Grade 1 Intervention | Grade 2 Intervention | Grade 3 Intervention | Grades 4–6 Intervention |
|---|---|---|---|---|---|
| **Phonics and Word Recognition (PWR)** | | | | | |
| Blending Sounds (consonants and vowels) | PWR, Lessons 1–52 | PA, Lesson 5 PWR, Lessons 1–87 | PA, Lesson 5 PWR, Lessons 1–122 | PWR, Lessons 41–44, 51 | N/A |
| Silent Letters | N/A | PWR, Lesson 28 | PWR, Lesson 22, 72 | PWR, Lesson 69 | N/A |
| High-frequency words | PWR, Lessons 1–48 | PWR, Lessons 1–31, 41–87 | PWR, Lessons 1–5, 7–9, 11–17, 19–23, 41–48, 51–70, 72–122 | N/A | N/A |
| Syllable Patterns (open, closed, vowel team patterns) | N/A | PWR, Lessons 17–21, 25–27, 29–31 | PWR, Lessons 3–5, 6, 7, 8, 16, 17, 19–20, 64, 68–70, 73–75 | PWR, Lessons 3, 10, 34–37, 50, 62 | PWR, Lessons 2, 3, 7–11 |
| Noun Plurals (regular and irregular) | PWR, Lesson 49 | PWR, Lesson 32, 35 | PWR, Lesson 6, 18, 23, 40 | PWR, Lesson 12 | PWR, Lesson 1 |
| Words with Inflectional Endings | PWR, Lesson 49 | PWR, Lessons 32–35 | PWR, Lesson 6, 10, 18, 25, 49, 50, 71 | PWR, Lessons 11, 37, 48, 49 | N/A |
| Words with Prefixes | PWR, Lesson 51 | PWR, Lesson 37 | PWR, Lessons 27–31 | PWR, Lessons 19–20, 22–24 | PWR, Lessons 14–15, 19–21, 23–25 |
| Words with Suffixes | PWR, Lesson 50, 52 | PWR, Lessons 38–40 | PWR, Lessons 24, 26, 32–40 | PWR, Lessons 9, 21, 25, 32, 38 | PWR, Lessons 12, 16–18, 22, 26–33 |
| Words with Greek Roots | N/A | N/A | N/A | N/A | N/A |
| **Fluency** | | | | | |
| On-level texts | N/A | Fluency Lessons 1a–4c | Fluency Lessons 1a–4c | Fluency Lessons 1a–4c | Fluency Lessons 1a–4c |

# LEVEL A

The Level A RF Screener has four parts. It may be administered to a small group, or the whole class. The chart below shows the part of the test; the number of questions, or items, in each part; and the estimated time for administering each part.

| Part of Test | Questions | Estimated Time |
|---|---|---|
| Letter Recognition | 1–5 | 5 minutes |
| Phonological Awareness | 1–5 | 5–10 minutes |
| Letter Sounds | 1–5 | 5–10 minutes |
| Word Recognition | 1–5 | 5 minutes |

## Level A Answer Key

| Letter Recognition | | Phonological Awareness | | Letter Sounds | | Word Recognition | |
|---|---|---|---|---|---|---|---|
| 1. | E | 1. | (seal) | 1. | k | 1. | see |
| 2. | N | 2. | (fish) | 2. | b | 2. | can |
| 3. | Y | 3. | (juice) | 3. | z | 3. | look |
| 4. | h | 4. | (rug) | 4. | l | 4. | my |
| 5. | r | 5. | (pin) | 5. | w | 5. | she |

To score the Level A test, use the Answer Key on this page. To use the Scoring Chart for Level A, go to page 12.

## Percentage Charts

| Part of Test | | | | | |
|---|---|---|---|---|---|
| Number Correct per part | 1 | 2 | 3 | 4 | 5 |
| Percent | 20 | 40 | 60 | 80 | 100 |

| Total Test | | | | | | | | | | | | | | | | | | | | |
|---|---|---|---|---|---|---|---|---|---|---|---|---|---|---|---|---|---|---|---|---|
| Number Correct | 1 | 2 | 3 | 4 | 5 | 6 | 7 | 8 | 9 | 10 | 11 | 12 | 13 | 14 | 15 | 16 | 17 | 18 | 19 | 20 |
| Percent | 5 | 10 | 15 | 20 | 25 | 30 | 35 | 40 | 45 | 50 | 55 | 60 | 65 | 70 | 75 | 80 | 85 | 90 | 95 | 100 |

# Scoring Chart

Student Name _____ Date _____

Teacher Name _____ Class _____

| Part of Test | Number Correct | Percent Score (%) |
|---|---|---|
| Letter Recognition<br>1　　2　　3　　4　　5 | /5 | |
| Phonological Awareness<br>1　　2　　3　　4　　5 | /5 | |
| Letter Sounds<br>1　　2　　3　　4　　5 | /5 | |
| Word Recognition<br>1　　2　　3　　4　　5 | /5 | |
| **Total Test** | **/20** | |
| Notes/Comments | | |
| Placement/Diagnosis | | |

# Scoring Chart

Student Name _____ Date _____

Teacher Name _____ Class _____

| Part of Test | Number Correct | Percent Score (%) |
|---|---|---|
| Letter Recognition<br>1　　2　　3　　4　　5 | /5 | |
| Phonological Awareness<br>1　　2　　3　　4　　5 | /5 | |
| Letter Sounds<br>1　　2　　3　　4　　5 | /5 | |
| Word Recognition<br>1　　2　　3　　4　　5 | /5 | |
| **Total Test** | **/20** | |
| Notes/Comments | | |
| Placement/Diagnosis | | |

# LEVEL B

The Level B RF Screener Test has five parts. It may be administered to an individual, to a small group, or to the whole class. The chart below shows the parts of the test; the number of questions, or items, in each part; and the estimated time for administering each part.

| Part of Test | Questions | Estimated Time |
|---|---|---|
| Letter Recognition | 1–5 | 5 minutes |
| Letter Sounds | 1–5 | 5–10 minutes |
| Consonants | 1–5 | 5–10 minutes |
| Vowel Sounds | 1–5 | 5–10 minutes |
| Word Recognition | 1-5 | 5 minutes |

## Level B Answer Key

| Letter Recognition | | Letter Sounds | | Consonants | | Vowel | | Word Recognition | |
|---|---|---|---|---|---|---|---|---|---|
| 1. | V | 1. | h | 1. | run | 1. | jet | 1. | now |
| 2. | I | 2. | c | 2. | quit | 2. | pack | 2. | could |
| 3. | q | 3. | f | 3. | block | 3. | bug | 3. | many |
| 4. | h | 4. | wed | 4. | wax | 4. | line | 4. | were |
| 5. | o | 5. | sum | 5. | mash | 5. | road | 5. | small |

To score the Level B test, use the Answer Key on this page. To use the Scoring Chart for Level B, go to page 14.

## Percentage Charts

| Part of Test | | | | | |
|---|---|---|---|---|---|
| Number Correct per part | 1 | 2 | 3 | 4 | 5 |
| Percent | 20 | 40 | 60 | 80 | 100 |

| Total Test | | | | | | | | | | | | | | | | | | | | | | | | | |
|---|---|---|---|---|---|---|---|---|---|---|---|---|---|---|---|---|---|---|---|---|---|---|---|---|---|
| Number Correct | 1 | 2 | 3 | 4 | 5 | 6 | 7 | 8 | 9 | 10 | 11 | 12 | 13 | 14 | 15 | 16 | 17 | 18 | 19 | 20 | 21 | 22 | 23 | 24 | 25 |
| Percent | 4 | 8 | 12 | 16 | 20 | 24 | 28 | 32 | 36 | 40 | 44 | 48 | 52 | 56 | 60 | 64 | 68 | 72 | 76 | 80 | 84 | 88 | 92 | 96 | 100 |

# Scoring Chart

Student Name _____ Date _____

Teacher Name _____ Class _____

| Part of Test | Number Correct | Percent Score (%) |
|---|---|---|
| Letter Recognition<br> 1    2    3    4    5 | /5 | |
| Letter Sounds<br> 1    2    3    4    5 | /5 | |
| Consonants<br> 1    2    3    4    5 | /5 | |
| Vowel Sounds<br> 1    2    3    4    5 | /5 | |
| Word Recognition<br> 1    2    3    4    5 | /5 | |
| **Total Test** | **/25** | . |
| Notes/Comments | | |
| Placement/Diagnosis | | |

# Scoring Chart

Student Name _____ Date _____

Teacher Name _____ Class _____

| Part of Test | Number Correct | Percent Score (%) |
|---|---|---|
| Letter Recognition<br> 1    2    3    4    5 | /5 | |
| Letter Sounds<br> 1    2    3    4    5 | /5 | |
| Consonants<br> 1    2    3    4    5 | /5 | |
| Vowel Sounds<br> 1    2    3    4    5 | /5 | |
| Word Recognition<br> 1    2    3    4    5 | /5 | |
| **Total Test** | **/25** | |
| Notes/Comments | | |
| Placement/Diagnosis | | |

# LEVEL C

The Level C RF Screener Test has four parts, as described in the chart. It may be administered to an individual, to a small group, or to the whole class. The chart below shows the parts of the test; the number of questions, or items, in each part; and the estimated time for administering each part

| Part of Test | Questions | Estimated Time |
|---|---|---|
| Consonants | 1–10 | 10 minutes |
| Vowels | 1–10 | 10 minutes |
| Word Recognition | 1–5 | 5–10 minutes |
| Word Study Skills | 1–5 | 5–10 minutes |

## Level C Answer Key

| Consonants | | | Vowels | | | Word Recognition | | | Word Study Skills | | |
|---|---|---|---|---|---|---|---|---|---|---|---|
| 1. | B (yet) | | 1. | B (fail) | | 1. | C (play) | | 1. | C (bunches) | |
| 2. | C (coat) | | 2. | A (look) | | 2. | D (buys) | | 2. | B (painting) | |
| 3. | A (gem) | | 3. | C (prime) | | 3. | C (carry) | | 3. | A (pennies) | |
| 4. | A (tray) | | 4. | A (flew) | | 4. | B (follow) | | 4. | C (their) | |
| 5. | B (know) | | 5. | B (punt) | | 5. | A (eight) | | 5. | C (hottest) | |
| 6. | A (buzz) | | 6. | C (grave) | | | | | | | |
| 7. | B (dusk) | | 7. | B (farm) | | | | | | | |
| 8. | C (lace) | | 8. | C (house) | | | | | | | |
| 9. | B (much) | | 9. | A (stalk) | | | | | | | |
| 10. | C (lamb) | | 10. | B (chair) | | | | | | | |

To score the Level C test, use the Answer Key on this page. To use the Scoring Chart for Level C, go to page 16.

## Percentage Charts

| Part of Test | | | | | Part of Test | | | | | | | | | |
|---|---|---|---|---|---|---|---|---|---|---|---|---|---|---|
| Number Correct per part | 1 | 2 | 3 | 4 | 5 | 1 | 2 | 3 | 4 | 5 | 6 | 7 | 8 | 9 | 10 |
| Percent | 20 | 40 | 60 | 80 | 100 | 10 | 20 | 30 | 40 | 50 | 60 | 70 | 80 | 90 | 100 |

| Total Test | | | | | | | | | | | | | | | | | | | | | | | | | | | | | |
|---|---|---|---|---|---|---|---|---|---|---|---|---|---|---|---|---|---|---|---|---|---|---|---|---|---|---|---|---|---|
| Number Correct | 1 | 2 | 3 | 4 | 5 | 6 | 7 | 8 | 9 | 10 | 11 | 12 | 13 | 14 | 15 | 16 | 17 | 18 | 19 | 20 | 21 | 22 | 23 | 24 | 25 | 26 | 27 | 28 | 29 | 30 |
| Percent | 3 | 7 | 10 | 13 | 17 | 20 | 23 | 27 | 30 | 33 | 37 | 40 | 43 | 47 | 50 | 53 | 57 | 60 | 63 | 67 | 70 | 73 | 77 | 80 | 83 | 87 | 90 | 93 | 97 | 100 |

# Scoring Chart

Student Name _____ Date _____

Teacher Name _____ Class _____

| Part of Test | Number Correct | Percent Score (%) |
|---|---|---|
| Consonants<br>1    2    3    4    5<br>6    7    8    9    10 | /10 | |
| Vowels<br>1    2    3    4    5<br>6    7    8    9    10 | /10 | |
| Word Recognition<br>1    2    3    4    5 | /5 | |
| Word Study Skills<br>1    2    3    4    5 | /5 | |
| **Total Test** | **/30** | |
| Notes/Comments | | |
| Placement/Diagnosis | | |

# Scoring Chart

Student Name _____ Date _____

Teacher Name _____ Class _____

| Part of Test | Number Correct | Percent Score (%) |
|---|---|---|
| Consonants<br>1    2    3    4    5<br>6    7    8    9    10 | /10 | |
| Vowels<br>1    2    3    4    5<br>6    7    8    9    10 | /10 | |
| Word Recognition<br>1    2    3    4    5 | /5 | |
| Word Study Skills<br>1    2    3    4    5 | /5 | |
| **Total Test** | **/30** | |
| Notes/Comments | | |
| Placement/Diagnosis | | |

*Today, I am going to ask you some questions. Listen carefully to each question. Then draw a circle around the answer. Let's begin.*

LETTER RECOGNITION

**I am going to say a letter. I want you to draw a circle around the letter I say. We will do a practice question first. Listen.**

SAMPLE

*Find the black dot at the top of the page. Put your finger on the dot. Look at the letters in the row. Draw a circle around the letter B . . . B.* (PAUSE) *Which letter is B?* (HAVE A STUDENT POINT TO THE B.) *Yes, that is the letter B. You should have drawn a circle around the B.*

*Now we will do some more questions like this.*

1. Move to the next row where you see the apple.
   Look at the letters in the row. Draw a circle around the letter E . . . E.

2. Move to the next row where you see the bell.
   Look at the letters in the row. Circle the letter N . . . N.

3. Move to the next row where you see the truck.
   Look at the letters in the row. Circle the letter Y . . . Y.

4. Move to the next row where you see the pencil.
   Look at the letters in the row. Circle the letter h . . . h.

5. Move to the next row where you see the boot.
   Look at the letters in the row. Circle the letter r . . . r.

PHONOLOGICAL AWARENESS

*Now I am going to ask you about beginning sounds. Listen to the word I say. Then look at the pictures. Find the picture that begins with the same sound as I say. We will do a practice question first. Listen.*

SAMPLE

*Find the black dot at the top of the page. Put your finger on the dot. Look at the pictures in the row: boy, mop, net. Which picture begins with the same sound as <u>men</u> . . . <u>men</u>? Draw a circle around the picture.* (PAUSE) *Which picture begins with the same sound as <u>men</u>?* (HAVE A STUDENT POINT TO THE SECOND PICTURE, MOP.) *Yes, the second picture is a <u>mop</u>. It begins with the same sound as <u>men</u>. You should have drawn a circle around the picture of a mop.*

*Now we will do some more questions like this.*

1. *Move to the next row, where you see the spoon. Look at the pictures in the row: cat, turtle, seal. Which begins with the same sound as <u>sit</u> . . . <u>sit</u>? Draw a circle around the picture.*

2. *Move to the next row, where you see the banana. Look at the pictures in the row: fish, pool, van. Which begins with the same sound as <u>five</u> . . . <u>five</u>? Circle the picture.*

3. *Move to the next row, where you see the chair. Look at the pictures in the row: lock, juice, kite. Which begins with the same sound as <u>joke</u> . . . <u>joke</u>? Circle the picture.*

*Now we will do something a little different. I am going to ask you about rhyming words. Turn to the next page. Find the black dot at the top of the page. Put your finger on the dot. Look at the pictures in the row: cap, cage, tie. Which picture rhymes with <u>tap</u> . . . <u>tap</u>? Draw a circle around the picture.* (PAUSE) *Which picture rhymes with tap?* (HAVE A STUDENT POINT TO THE FIRST PICTURE, <u>CAP</u>.) *Yes, the first picture is a <u>cap</u>. It rhymes with <u>tap</u>. You should have drawn a circle around the picture of a cap.*

*Now we will do some more questions like this.*

4. *Move to the next row, where you see the mittens. Look at the pictures in the row: bat, dog, rug. Which picture rhymes with <u>bug</u> . . . <u>bug</u>? Circle the picture.*

5. *Move to the next row, where you see the umbrella. Look at the pictures in the row: nine, whale, pin. Which picture rhymes with <u>win</u> . . . <u>win</u>? Circle the picture.*

LETTER SOUNDS

*Now I am going to ask you about letter sounds. Listen to the word I say. Then look at the letters in the row. Find the letter for the beginning sound in the word. Listen.*

SAMPLE

*Find the black dot at the top of the page where you see the picture of the sun. Put your finger on the dot. Look at the letters in the row. Find the letter for the beginning sound of <u>sun</u> . . . <u>sun</u>. Draw a circle around the letter.* (PAUSE) *Which letter makes the beginning sound of <u>sun</u>?* (HAVE A STUDENT POINT TO THE S.) *Yes, the letter <u>s</u> makes the beginning sound of the word <u>sun</u>. You should have drawn a circle around the <u>s</u>.*

*Now we will do some more questions like this.*

1. *Move to the next row, where you see the picture of the key. Look at the letters in the row. Find the letter for the beginning sound of <u>key</u> . . . <u>key</u>. Draw a circle around the letter.*

2. *Move to the next row, where you see the picture of the bed. Look at the letters in the row. Find the letter for the beginning sound of <u>bed</u> . . . <u>bed</u>. Circle the letter.*

3. *Move to the next row, where you see the picture of the zebra. Look at the letters in the row. Find the letter for the beginning sound of <u>zebra</u> . . . <u>zebra</u>. Circle the letter.*

4. *Move to the next row, where you see the picture of the lemon. Look at the letters in the row. Find the letter for the beginning sound of <u>lemon</u> . . . <u>lemon</u>. Circle the letter.*

5. *Move to the next row, where you see the picture of the wagon. Look at the letters in the row. Find the letter for the beginning sound of <u>wagon</u> . . . <u>wagon</u>. Circle the letter.*

WORD RECOGNITION

*Now I am going to ask you to find some words.*

SAMPLE

*Find the black dot at the top of the page. Put your finger on the dot. Look at the words in the row. Listen as I read the words: I like it. Draw a circle around the word <u>like</u> . . . <u>like</u>.* (PAUSE) *Which word is <u>like</u>?* (HAVE A STUDENT POINT TO THE WORD <u>LIKE</u>.) *Yes, the second word is <u>like</u>. You should have drawn a circle around the word <u>like</u>.*

*Now we will do some more questions like this.*

1. *Move to the next row, where you see the picture of the apple. Look at the words in the row: We see you. Draw a circle around the word <u>see</u> . . . <u>see</u>.*

2. *Move to the next row, where you see the picture of the bell. Look at the words in the row: He can jump. Circle the word <u>can</u> . . . <u>can</u>.*

3. *Move to the next row, where you see the picture of the truck. Look at the words in the row: Look at the little bug. Circle the word <u>look</u> . . . <u>look</u>.*

4. *Move to the next row, where you see the picture of the pencil. Look at the words in the row: This is my pet. Circle the word <u>my</u> . . . <u>my</u>.*

5. *Move to the next row, where you see the picture of the boot. Look at the words in the row: She has two hats. Circle the word <u>she</u> . . . <u>she</u>.*

Name _____ Date _____

# Level A: Letter Recognition

●

| I | B | O | F |
|---|---|---|---|

---

1.

| E | L | G | C |
|---|---|---|---|

---

2.

| D | N | M | A |
|---|---|---|---|

## Level A: Letter Recognition

3.

J          X          Y          Z

4.

h          k          k          b

5.

t          v          u          r

Name _____  Date _____

# Level A: Phonological Awareness

**1.**

**2.**

**3.**

# Level A: Phonological Awareness

●

---

**4.**

---

**5.**

**9**   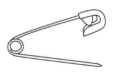

# Level A: Letter Sounds

●

c          s          n

---

1.

k          t          y

---

2.

d          p          b

## Level A: Letter Sounds

3.

y        z        s

4.

l        h        j

5.

m        v        w

Name _____ Date _____

## Level A: Word Recognition

● 

I like it.

1.

We see you.

2.

He can jump.

## Level A: Word Recognition

3.

# Look at the little bug.

---

4.

# This is my pet.

---

5.

# She has two hats.

*Today, I am going to ask you some questions. Listen carefully to each question. Then draw a circle around the answer. Let's begin.*

LETTER RECOGNITION

*I am going to say a letter. I want you to draw a circle around the letter I say. We will do a practice question first. Listen.*

SAMPLE

*Find the black dot at the top of the page. Put your finger on the dot. Look at the letters in the row. Circle the letter A . . . A.* (PAUSE) *Which letter is A?* (HAVE A STUDENT POINT TO THE A.) *Yes, that is the letter A. You should have drawn a circle around the A.*

*Now we will do some more questions like this.*

1. Move to the next row, where you see the number 1. Look at the letters in the row. Circle the letter V . . . V.

2. Move to the next row, where you see the number 2. Look at the letters in the row. Circle the letter I . . . I.

3. Move to the next row, where you see the number 3. Look at the letters in the row. Circle the letter q . . . q.

4. Move to the next row, where you see the number 4. Look at the letters in the row. Circle the letter h . . . h.

5. Move to the next row, where you see the number 5. Look at the letters in the row. Circle the letter o . . . o.

LETTER SOUNDS

*Now I am going to ask you about beginning sounds. Listen to the word I say. Then look at the letters. Find the letter for the beginning sound of the word I say. We will do a practice question first. Listen.*

SAMPLE

*Find the black dot at the top of the page. Put your finger on the dot. Look at the letters in the row. Find the letter for the beginning sound of <u>road</u> . . . <u>road</u>. Draw a circle around the letter.* (PAUSE) *Which letter makes the beginning sound of <u>road</u>?* (HAVE A STUDENT POINT TO THE R.) *Yes, the letter r makes the beginning sound of the word <u>road</u>. You should have drawn a circle around the r.*

*Now we will do some more questions like this.*

1. *Move to the next row, where you see the number 1.*
   *Look at the letters in the row. Find the letter for the beginning sound of <u>honey</u> . . . <u>honey</u>. Draw a circle around the letter.*

2. *Move to the next row, where you see the number 2.*
   *Look at the letters in the row. Find the letter for the beginning sound of <u>carrot</u> . . . <u>carrot</u>. Circle the letter.*

3. *Move to the next row, where you see the number 3.*
   *Look at the letters in the row. Find the letter for the beginning sound of <u>feather</u> . . . <u>feather</u>.*

*Now we will do something a little different. I am going to ask you about rhyming words. Turn to the next page. Find the black dot at the top of the page. Put your finger on the dot. Look at the words in the row. Which word rhymes with <u>lip</u> . . . <u>lip</u>? Draw a circle around the word.* (PAUSE) *Which word rhymes with <u>lip</u>?* (HAVE A STUDENT POINT TO THE WORD SIP.) *Yes, the first word is <u>sip</u>. It rhymes with <u>lip</u>. You should have drawn a circle around the word <u>sip</u>.*
*Now we will do some more questions like this.*

4. *Move to the next row, where you see the number 4.*
   *Look at the words in the row. Which word rhymes with <u>bed</u> . . . <u>bed</u>? Circle the word.*

5. *Move to the next row, where you see the number 5.*
   *Look at the words in the row. Which word rhymes with <u>hum</u> . . . <u>hum</u>? Circle the word.*

## CONSONANTS

*Now I am going to ask you about words with the same beginning sound. Listen to the word I say. Then look at the words in the row. Find the word with the same beginning sound. Listen.*

## SAMPLE

*Find the black dot at the top of the page. Put your finger on the dot. Look at the words in the row. Find the word that has the same beginning sound as <u>window</u> . . . <u>window</u>. Draw a circle around the word.* (PAUSE) **Which word has the same beginning sound as <u>window</u>?** (HAVE A STUDENT POINT TO THE WORD <u>WET</u>.) **Yes, the word <u>wet</u> has the same beginning sound as <u>window</u>. You should have drawn a circle around <u>wet</u>.**

*Now we will do some more questions like this.*

1. *Move to the next row, where you see the number 1. Look at the words in the row. Which word has the same beginning sound as <u>rake</u> . . . <u>rake</u>? Circle the word.*

2. *Move to the next row, where you see the number 2. Look at the words in the row. Which word has the same beginning sound as <u>queen</u> . . . <u>queen</u>? Circle the word.*

3. *Move to the next row, where you see the number 3. Look at the words in the row. Which word has the same beginning sounds as <u>blanket</u> . . . <u>blanket</u>? Circle the word.*

*Now we will do something a little different. I am going to ask you about words with the same ending sound. Listen to the word I say. Then look at the words in the row. Find the word with the same ending sound. Listen.*

SAMPLE

*Find the black dot at the top of the next page. Put your finger on the dot. Look at the words in the row. Find the word that has the same ending sound as* <u>log</u> *. . .* <u>log</u>. *Draw a circle around the word.* (PAUSE) *Which word has the same ending sound as* <u>log</u>? (HAVE A STUDENT POINT TO THE WORD <u>FIG</u>.) *Yes, the word* <u>fig</u> *has the same ending sound as* <u>log</u>.
*You should have drawn a circle around* <u>fig</u>.

*Now we will do some more questions like this.*

4. *Move to the next row, where you see the number 4. Look at the words in the row. Circle the word with the same ending sound as* <u>six</u> *. . .* <u>six</u>.
5. *Move to the next row, where you see the number 5. Look at the words in the row. Circle the word with the same ending sound as* <u>fish</u> *. . .* <u>fish</u>.

<u>VOWEL SOUNDS</u>

*Now I am going to ask you about vowel sounds. Listen to the word I say. Then look at the words in the row. Find the word with the same vowel sound. Listen.*

<u>SAMPLE</u>

*Find the black dot at the top of the page. Put your finger on the dot. Look at the words in the row. Which word has the same vowel sound as <u>lot</u> . . . <u>lot</u>? Draw a circle around the word.* (PAUSE) ***Which word has the same vowel sound as <u>lot</u>?*** (HAVE A STUDENT POINT TO THE WORD <u>COB</u>.) ***Yes, the word <u>cob</u> has the same vowel sound as <u>lot</u>. The vowel sound is the sound in the middle of the word. You should have drawn a circle around <u>cob</u>.***

*Now we will do some more questions like this.*

1. *Move to the next row, where you see the number 1. Look at the words in the row. Which word has the same vowel sound as <u>den</u> . . . <u>den</u>? Circle the word.*

2. *Move to the next row, where you see the number 2. Look at the words in the row. Which word has the same vowel sound as <u>sad</u> . . . <u>sad</u>? Circle the word.*

3. *Move to the next row, where you see the number 3. Look at the words in the row. Which word has the same vowel sound as <u>run</u> . . . <u>run</u>? Circle the word.*

4. *Move to the next row, where you see the number 4. Look at the words in the row. Which word has the same vowel sound as <u>right</u> . . . <u>right</u>? Circle the word.*

5. *Move to the next row, where you see the number 5. Look at the words in the row. Which word has the same vowel sound as <u>go</u> . . . <u>go</u>? Circle the word.*

WORD RECOGNITION

*Now I am going to ask you to find some words.*

SAMPLE

*Find the black dot at the top of the page. Put your finger on the dot. Look at the words in the row. Listen as I read the words: She can jump. Draw a circle around the word <u>can</u> . . . <u>can</u>.* (PAUSE) **Which word is <u>can</u>?** (HAVE A STUDENT POINT TO THE WORD <u>CAN</u>.) **Yes, the second word is <u>can</u>, c-a-n. You should have drawn a circle around the word <u>can</u>.**

*Now we will do some more questions like this.*

1. *Move to the next row, where you see the number 1. Look at the words in the row: Nell is here now. Circle the word <u>now</u> . . . <u>now</u>.*

2. *Move to the next row, where you see the number 2. Look at the words in the row: Dad said you could go. Circle the word <u>could</u> . . . <u>could</u>.*

3. *Move to the next row, where you see the number 3. Look at the words in the row: How many do you have? Circle the word <u>many</u> . . . <u>many</u>.*

4. *Move to the next row, where you see the number 4. Look at the words in the row: We were playing a game. Circle the word <u>were</u> . . . <u>were</u>.*

5. *Move to the next row, where you see the number 5. Look at the words in the row: Look at the small brown dog. Circle the word <u>small</u> . . . <u>small</u>.*

Name _____ Date _____

# Level B: Letter Recognition

●

D    C    A    X

_____

1.

W    N    M    V

_____

2.

T    I    Z    S

## Level B: Letter Recognition

**3.**

q        j        g        p

_____

**4.**

k        t        h        l

_____

**5.**

b        o        p        e

# Level B: Letter Sounds

●

       d       r       w

1.

       y       n       h

2.

       r       c       t

3.

       f       p       v

## Level B: Letter Sounds

●

sip           lid           sap

**4.**

wet          wed         bad

**5.**

ram         him        sum

## Level B: Consonants

- 
   **met**     **wet**     **vet**

1.

   **run**     **sun**     **fun**

2.

   **wit**     **pit**     **quit**

3.

   **flock**     **clock**     **block**

## Level B: Consonants

● 

**fit**       **fin**       **fig**

---

**4.**

**wag**       **wax**       **was**

---

**5.**

**mash**       **mast**       **mask**

## Level B: Vowel Sounds

●

cab        cub        cob

1.

jet        jot        jut

2.

pick        pack        peck

## Level B: Vowel Sounds

**3.**

**bag**         **beg**         **bug**

---

**4.**

**line**         **lane**         **lone**

---

**5.**

**rod**         **road**         **red**

## Level B: Word Recognition

- **She can jump.**

1. **Nell is here now.**

2. **Dad said you could go.**

3. **How many do you have?**

4. **We were playing a game.**

5. **Look at the small brown dog.**

*Today, I am going to ask you some questions. Listen carefully to each question. Then fill in the bubble beside the answer. Let's begin.*

CONSONANTS

*I am going to ask you about words with the same beginning sound. Listen to the word I say. Then look at the words in the row. Find the word with the same beginning sound. Listen.*

SAMPLE

*Find the black dot at the top of the page. Look at the words in the row. Which word has the same beginning sound as <u>fall</u> . . . <u>fall</u>? Fill in the bubble beside the word.* (PAUSE) *Which word has the same beginning sound as <u>fall</u>?* (HAVE A STUDENT SAY OR POINT TO THE WORD <u>FAN</u>.) *Yes, <u>fan</u> has the same beginning sound as <u>fall</u>. You should have filled in the bubble beside f<u>an</u>.*

*Now we will do some more questions like this.*

1. *Move to the next row, where you see the number 1. Look at the words in the row. Which word has the same beginning sound as <u>yarn</u> . . . <u>yarn</u>? Fill in the bubble.*

2. *Move to the next row, where you see the number 2. Look at the words in the row. Which word has the same beginning sound as <u>king</u> . . . <u>king</u>? Fill in the bubble.*

3. *Move to the next row, where you see the number 3. Look at the words in the row. Fill in the bubble beside the word with the same beginning sound as <u>jacket</u> . . . <u>jacket.</u>*

4. *Move to the next row, number 4. Look at the words in the row. Fill in the bubble beside the word with the same beginning sounds as <u>tree</u> . . . <u>tree</u>.*

5. *Move to the next row, number 5. Look at the words in the row. Fill in the bubble beside the word with the same beginning sound as <u>nice</u> . . . <u>nice</u>.*

*Now we will do something a little different. I am going to ask you about words with the same ending sound. Listen to the word I say. Then look at the words in the row. Find the word with the same ending sound. Listen.*

SAMPLE

*Find the next black dot. Look at the words in the row. Which word has the same ending sound as <u>plain</u> . . . <u>plain</u>? Fill in the bubble beside the word.* (PAUSE) *Which word has the same ending sound as <u>plain</u>?* (HAVE A STUDENT SAY OR POINT TO THE WORD <u>SEEN</u>.) *Yes, <u>seen</u> has the same ending sound as <u>plain</u>. You should have filled in the bubble beside <u>seen</u>.*

*Now we will do some more questions like this.*

6. *Move to the next row, number 6. Look at the words in the row. Which word has the same ending sound as <u>fizz</u> . . . <u>fizz</u>? Fill in the bubble.*

7. *Move to row 7. Look at the words. Fill in the bubble beside the word with the same ending sounds as <u>mask</u> . . . <u>mask</u>.*

8. *Move to row 8. Look at the words. Fill in the bubble beside the word with the same ending sound as <u>rice</u> . . . <u>rice</u>.*

9. *Move to row 9. Look at the words. Fill in the bubble beside the word with the same ending sound as <u>teach</u> . . . <u>teach</u>.*

10. *Move to row 10. Look at the words. Fill in the bubble beside the word with the same ending sound as <u>climb</u>. . . <u>climb</u>.*

VOWELS

*Now I am going to ask you about vowel sounds. Listen to the word I say. Then look at the words in the row. Find the word with the same vowel sound. Listen.*

SAMPLE

*Find the black dot at the top of the page. Look at the words in the row. Which word has the same vowel sound as <u>grow</u> . . . <u>grow</u>? Fill in the bubble beside the word.* (PAUSE) *Which word has the same vowel sound as <u>grow</u>?* (HAVE A STUDENT SAY OR POINT TO THE WORD <u>ROSE</u>.) *Yes, <u>rose</u> has the same vowel sound as <u>grow.</u> You should have filled in the bubble beside <u>rose.</u>*

*Now we will do some more questions like this.*

(For this set of questions, say the number before reading the question.)

1. *Which word has the same vowel sound as <u>take</u> . . . <u>take</u>? Fill in the bubble.*

2. *Which word has the same vowel sound as <u>hood</u> . . . <u>hood</u>? Fill in the bubble.*

3. *Which word has the same vowel sound as <u>vine</u> . . . <u>vine</u>? Fill in the bubble.*

4. *Fill in the bubble beside the word with the same vowel sound as <u>glue</u> . . . <u>glue</u>.*

5. *Fill in the bubble beside the word with the same vowel sound as <u>duck</u> . . . <u>duck</u>.*

6. *Which word has the same vowel sound as <u>rain</u> . . . <u>rain</u>? Fill in the bubble.*

7. *Fill in the bubble beside the word with the same vowel sound as <u>dark</u> . . . <u>dark</u>.*

8. *Fill in the bubble beside the word with the same vowel sound as <u>now</u> . . . <u>now</u>.*

9. *Fill in the bubble beside the word with the same vowel sound as <u>call</u> . . . <u>call</u>.*

10. *Fill in the bubble beside the word with the same vowel sound as <u>where</u> . . . <u>where</u>.*

<u>WORD RECOGNITION</u>

*Now I am going to ask you to find some words.*

<u>SAMPLE</u>

*Find the black dot at the top of the page. Look at the sentence in the row. Read the sentence to yourself and find the word <u>like</u>. Fill in the bubble under the word <u>like</u>.* (PAUSE) *Which bubble did you fill in?* (HAVE A STUDENT SAY OR POINT TO THE BUBBLE FOR ANSWER C, <u>LIKE</u>.) *Yes, that is the word <u>like</u>. You should have filled in the bubble for answer C.*

*Now we will do some more questions like this.*

(For this set of questions, read the number before reading the question.)

1. *Read the sentence and find the word <u>play</u>. Fill in the bubble under the word <u>play</u>.*

2. *Read the sentence and find the word <u>buys</u>. Fill in the bubble under the word <u>buys</u>.*

3. *Read the sentence and find the word <u>carry</u>. Fill in the bubble under the word <u>carry</u>.*

4. *Read the sentence and find the word <u>follow</u>. Fill in the bubble under the word <u>follow</u>.*

5. *Read the sentence and find the word <u>eight</u>. Fill in the bubble under the word <u>eight</u>.*

WORD STUDY SKILLS

*In this part, each question shows a sentence with a blank. You will read the sentence and choose the correct word to complete the sentence. We will start with a practice question.*

SAMPLE

*Find the black dot at the top of the page. Read the sentence and find the correct word to complete the sentence. Fill in the bubble beside the answer.* (PAUSE) *Which is the correct word to complete the sentence?* (HAVE A STUDENT SAY OR POINT TO THE WORD SHELLS, ANSWER B.) *Yes, the correct word is* shells, *answer B. "We found five shells." You should have filled in the bubble for answer B.*

*Now you will do the rest of the questions on this page in the same way. Read the sentence. Then choose the correct word to complete the sentence. Fill in the bubble beside the answer you choose. You may begin.*

HAVE STUDENTS ANSWER QUESTIONS 1–5.

Name _____   Date _____

# Level C: Consonants

**Directions:** Listen to the word your teacher says. For numbers 1-5 find the word that has the same beginning sound. For numbers 6-10 find the word that has the same ending sound. Fill in the bubble beside the word.

| | | |
|---|---|---|
| • | ⓐ pan | ⓑ fan | ⓒ tan |
| 1. | ⓐ wet | ⓑ yet | ⓒ vet |
| 2. | ⓐ boat | ⓑ goat | ⓒ coat |
| 3. | ⓐ gem | ⓑ hem | ⓒ stem |
| 4. | ⓐ tray | ⓑ pray | ⓒ gray |
| 5. | ⓐ snow | ⓑ know | ⓒ crow |
| • | ⓐ seen | ⓑ seed | ⓒ seem |
| 6. | ⓐ buzz | ⓑ bus | ⓒ bunch |
| 7. | ⓐ dust | ⓑ dusk | ⓒ duck |
| 8. | ⓐ late | ⓑ lake | ⓒ lace |
| 9. | ⓐ must | ⓑ much | ⓒ muck |
| 10. | ⓐ lamp | ⓑ long | ⓒ lamb |

Name _____ Date _____

## Level C: Vowels

**Directions:** Listen to the word your teacher says. Find the word that has the same vowel sound. Fill in the bubble beside the word.

| | | |
|---|---|---|
| • | ⓐ **rose** | ⓑ **raise** | ⓒ **rise** |
| 1. | ⓐ **feel** | ⓑ **fail** | ⓒ **foil** |
| 2. | ⓐ **look** | ⓑ **lock** | ⓒ **luck** |
| 3. | ⓐ **prom** | ⓑ **prim** | ⓒ **prime** |
| 4. | ⓐ **flew** | ⓑ **flaw** | ⓒ **flow** |
| 5. | ⓐ **pant** | ⓑ **punt** | ⓒ **point** |
| 6. | ⓐ **grove** | ⓑ **groove** | ⓒ **grave** |
| 7. | ⓐ **form** | ⓑ **farm** | ⓒ **firm** |
| 8. | ⓐ **horse** | ⓑ **hose** | ⓒ **house** |
| 9. | ⓐ **stalk** | ⓑ **stake** | ⓒ **stack** |
| 10. | ⓐ **cheer** | ⓑ **chair** | ⓒ **chore** |

Name _____ Date _____

# Level C: Word Recognition

**Directions:** Read the sentence. Find the word your teacher says. Fill in the bubble under the word.

---

● **Some people like to laugh.**

     (a)      (b)      (c)      (d)

---

**1.** **She wants to play a game.**

     (a)      (b)      (c)      (d)

---

**2.** **That boy always buys a snack.**

     (a)      (b)      (c)      (d)

---

**3.** **We can carry four boxes.**

     (a)      (b)      (c)      (d)

---

**4.** **I will follow her across the street.**

     (a)      (b)      (c)      (d)

---

**5.** **Eight girls walk to the school.**

     (a)      (b)      (c)      (d)

---

Name _____ Date _____

# Level C: Word Study Skills

**Directions:** Read the sentence. Choose the correct word to complete the sentence.
Fill in the bubble beside the word.

**We found five _____.**

● 
- Ⓐ shell
- Ⓑ shells
- Ⓒ shellses

**Danny ate two _____ of grapes.**

**1.**
- Ⓐ bunch
- Ⓑ bunchs
- Ⓒ bunches

**Grandma is _____ her house.**

**2.**
- Ⓐ painted
- Ⓑ painting
- Ⓒ paints

**Kendra picked up some _____.**

**3.**
- Ⓐ pennies
- Ⓑ pennys
- Ⓒ pennyes

**Sometimes I ride in _____ car.**

**4.**
- Ⓐ there
- Ⓑ they're
- Ⓒ their

**That was the _____ day of the summer.**

**5.**
- Ⓐ hotest
- Ⓑ hotter
- Ⓒ hottest

# Part 2: Table of Contents

## Section One: Print Concepts Quick Checks and Reading Observation Forms

**Teacher Pages:**

## Section Two: Phonological Awareness Quick Checks

**Teacher Pages:**

## Section Three: Phonics and Word Recognition Quick Checks

**Teacher Pages:**

**Student Pages:**

## Section Four: Fluency Quick Checks

**Teacher Pages:**

**Student Pages:**

## Print Concepts

The quick check in this section allows you to assess students' understanding of print concepts. There are also reading observation records to be used over a span of time to measure students' understanding about the reading process. These help measure understanding and growth in the areas of linking prior knowledge, reading for meaning, developing vocabulary, developing comprehension, and responding to the text. There are individual and small-group observation forms for each grade set (K–1 and 1–2).

### Reading Observation Records Administration

1. On a regular basis, schedule time to observe each student or small groups reading.

2. Copy the Individual Reading Observation Record or Small-Group Reading Observation Record form for each student's stage of development or grade level.

3. On each form, record the student(s') name(s) and the date.

4. Prior to the observation, read through the form to become familiar with the list of behaviors you may be observing while the student is reading.

5. Ask the student to read aloud from the text.

6. For each criterion, determine if the student is at the beginning, progressing, or proficient stage of reading development and check the column to indicate the stage.

7. Record any observations or comments made during the oral reading at the bottom of the page. If needed, conduct a brief interview for additional information regarding a student's understanding of particular reading behaviors.

8. After analyzing, place the Reading Observation Record in the appropriate organized storage location.

### Using the Results

After completing the observation records, review the form(s) to determine trends, patterns, and information that stands out about students' progression. If you notice a behavior that is at the beginning stage of development for most of your class, this can become a focus of whole-group lessons. The behaviors that stand out as individual concerns may be addressed in small-group or individualized lessons.

# Print Concepts Quick Check

Name _____  Date _____

| What to Ask | What to Look For | Results | |
|---|---|---|---|
| Where is the cover? | Student points to the cover. | ❑Yes | ❑No |
| Where is the title? | Student points to the title on the cover. | ❑Yes | ❑No |
| Where is the author's name? | Student points to the author's name on the cover. | ❑Yes | ❑No |
| How should I open the book? | Student correctly demonstrates how to open the book. | ❑Yes | ❑No |
| Where is the first page? | Student points to the title page. | ❑Yes | ❑No |
| Where is the top of the page? | Student points to the top of the page. | ❑Yes | ❑No |
| Where is the bottom of the page? | Student points to the bottom of the page. | ❑Yes | ❑No |
| (Turn to a spread.) Where are some words? | Student points to any words on the page. | ❑Yes | ❑No |
| Where is a picture? | Student points to a photo or drawing on the page. | ❑Yes | ❑No |
| Where should I start reading? | Student points to the first word on the page. | ❑Yes | ❑No |
| How should my finger move as I read? | Student moves finger from left to right under the line of print. | ❑Yes | ❑No |
| Can you point to the words as I read this line? | Student correctly demonstrates one-to-one matching as you read. | ❑Yes | ❑No |
| How many words are in this line? | Student correctly identifies the number of words in the line. | ❑Yes | ❑No |
| Where should I start reading next? | Student points to the first word on the second line of print. | ❑Yes | ❑No |
| Where is an uppercase letter on the page? | Student points to an uppercase letter at the beginning of any sentence. | ❑Yes | ❑No |
| Can you point to the first letter in a word? | Student points to the first letter in any word. | ❑Yes | ❑No |
| Can you point to the last letter in a word? | Student points to the last letter in any word. | ❑Yes | ❑No |
| (Point to a period on any page.) What is this punctuation mark? What does it mean? | Student says "period." Student says "It tells you stop because the sentence is done" or gives a similar explanation. | ❑Yes | ❑No |
| (Point to a question mark on any page.) What is this punctuation mark? What does it mean? | Student says "question mark." Student says "Someone is asking something" or gives a similar explanation. | ❑Yes | ❑No |
| (Point to an exclamation point on any page.) What is this punctuation mark? What does it mean? | Student says "exclamation point." Student says "It means you use an excited voice" or gives a similar explanation. | ❑Yes | ❑No |
| (Point to a comma on any page.) What is this punctuation mark? What does it mean?` | Student says "comma." Student says "It tells you to pause" or gives a similar explanation. | ❑Yes | ❑No |

# Individual Reading Observation Record • K–1

Name _____ Date _____ Text Title _____ Text Level _____

| Reading Behavior | Beginning | Progressing | Proficient |
|---|---|---|---|
| Reads fluently; problem-solves on one or two things only | | | |
| One-to-one matching | | | |
| Directionality | | | |
| Return sweep | | | |
| Knows a small core of high-frequency words that can be read fluently | | | |
| Self-monitors and attends to print, using high-frequency words | | | |
| Aware of errors and searches the picture as well as the print | | | |
| Rereads by returning to the beginning of the sentence | | | |
| Cross-checks prediction at point of difficulty with the picture and print | | | |
| Rereads at point of difficulty and articulates the first letter of the problem word | | | |
| **Comments/Concerns:** | | | |

Foundational Skills Assessments ©2017 Benchmark Education Company, LLC

# Individual Reading Observation Record • K–1 (continued)

Name _____ Date _____ Text Title _____ Text Level _____

| Reading Behavior | Beginning | Progressing | Proficient |
|---|---|---|---|
| Returns to reread closer to the point of difficulty | | | |
| Beginning to search through a difficult word for additional information by blending letters into sounds | | | |
| Fluently uses beginning chunks, or parts of words, and ending sounds | | | |
| Meaning and structure are guiding the reading | | | |
| Integrates meaning, structure, and visual cues; is moving towards automaticity | | | |
| Self-monitors; is moving toward automaticity | | | |
| Analyzes words using graphophonic patterns | | | |
| Reads high-frequency words fluently | | | |
| Recognizes errors when reading and initiates problem-solving actions | | | |
| **Comments/Concerns:** | | | |

# Individual Reading Observation Record • Grades 1–2

Name _____ Date _____ Text Title _____ Text Level _____

| Reading Behavior | Beginning | Progressing | Proficient |
|---|---|---|---|
| Reads fluently; problem-solves on one or two things only | | | |
| Problem-solves at the point of error and makes multiple attempts to self-correct | | | |
| Searches through the difficult word and blends sounds together | | | |
| Takes words apart using large units or syllables | | | |
| Meaning and structure guide the reading; uses visual information to check on reading | | | |
| Reads longer texts with greater accuracy | | | |
| Uses word meaning and context clues to problem-solve | | | |
| Increasing control of visual patterns and flexible use of strategies | | | |
| Reads high-frequency words fluently | | | |
| **Comments/Concerns:** | | | |

# Individual Reading Observation Record • Grades 1–2 (continued)

Name _____ Date _____ Text Title _____ Text Level _____

| Reading Behavior | Beginning | Progressing | Proficient |
|---|---|---|---|
| Uses nonfiction text features to locate information on a topic, including table of contents, headings, glossaries, boldfaced print, indices | | | |
| Interprets and uses nonfiction text features such as maps, charts, tables, flow charts, diagrams, time lines | | | |
| Decodes text using knowledge of common letter-sound correspondences, including blends, digraphs, consonant variants, r-controlled vowels, and a variety of spelling patterns | | | |
| Decodes text using knowledge of the structure of words such as endings, prefixes, suffixes, compound words, contractions, and root words | | | |
| Identifies variant sounds of consonants and vowels | | | |
| Integrates meaning, structure, and visual cues to decode and comprehend text | | | |
| Uses strategies of sampling, predicting, confirming, and self-correction independently | | | |
| Makes inferences from texts | | | |
| Reads longer, less-predictable texts with complex text structures | | | |
| Identifies nonfiction text structures such as descriptive, problem/solution, time order, compare/contrast, cause/effect, and directions | | | |
| **Comments/Concerns:** | | | |

# Small-Group Reading Observation Record • K–1

Date_____

Text Title_____

Text Level_____

Chart Coding Legend
* Proficent
✓ Progressing
X Beginning

| Student's Name | Reads fluently; problem-solves on one or two things only | One-to-one matching | Directionality | Return sweep | Knows a small core of high-frequency words that can be read fluently | Self-monitors and attends to print, using high-frequency words | Aware of errors and searches the picture as well as the print | Rereads by returning to the beginning of the sentence | Cross-checks prediction at point of difficulty with the picture and print | Rereads at point of difficulty and articulates the first letter of the problem word |
|---|---|---|---|---|---|---|---|---|---|---|
| | | | | | | | | | | |
| | | | | | | | | | | |
| | | | | | | | | | | |
| | | | | | | | | | | |
| | | | | | | | | | | |
| | | | | | | | | | | |

**Comments/Concerns**

_____

_____

_____

_____

_____

_____

_____

*Foundational Skills Assessments*

# Small-Group Reading Observation Record • K–1 (continued)

Date_____

Text Title_____

Text Level_____

Chart Coding Legend
* Proficent
✓ Progressing
X Beginning

| Student's Name | Reads fluently; problem-solves on one or two things only | Returns to reread closer to the point of difficulty | Beginning to search through a difficult word for additional information by blending letters into sounds | Fluently uses beginning chunks, or parts of words, and ending sounds | Meaning and structure are guiding the reading | Integrates meaning, structure, and visual cues; is moving toward automaticity | Self-monitors; is moving toward automaticity | Analyzes words using graphophonic patterns | Reads high-frequency words fluently | Recognizes errors when reading and initiates problem-solving actions |
|---|---|---|---|---|---|---|---|---|---|---|
|  |  |  |  |  |  |  |  |  |  |  |
|  |  |  |  |  |  |  |  |  |  |  |
|  |  |  |  |  |  |  |  |  |  |  |
|  |  |  |  |  |  |  |  |  |  |  |
|  |  |  |  |  |  |  |  |  |  |  |
|  |  |  |  |  |  |  |  |  |  |  |

## Comments/Concerns

_____

_____

_____

_____

_____

_____

# Small-Group Reading Observation Record • 1–2

Date _____

Text Title _____

Text Level _____

Chart Coding Legend

\* Proficent

✓ Progressing

X Beginning

| Student's Name | Reads fluently; problem-solves on one or two things only | Problem-solves at the point of error and makes multiple attempts to self-correct | Searches through the difficult word and blends sounds together | Takes words apart using large units or syllables | Meaning and structure guide the reading; uses visual information to check on reading | Reads longer texts with greater accuracy | Uses word meaning and context clues to problem-solve | Increasing control of visual patterns and flexible use of strategies | Reads high-frequency words fluently |
|---|---|---|---|---|---|---|---|---|---|
|  |  |  |  |  |  |  |  |  |  |
|  |  |  |  |  |  |  |  |  |  |
|  |  |  |  |  |  |  |  |  |  |
|  |  |  |  |  |  |  |  |  |  |
|  |  |  |  |  |  |  |  |  |  |
|  |  |  |  |  |  |  |  |  |  |

**Comments/Concerns**

_____

_____

_____

_____

_____

_____

_____

*Foundational Skills Assessments*

# Small-Group Reading Observation Record • 1–2 (continued)

Date _____

Text Title _____

Text Level _____

Chart Coding Legend
* Proficent
✓ Progressing
X Beginning

**Student's Name**

| | Uses nonfiction text features to locate information on a topic, including table of contents, headings, glossaries, boldfaced print, indices | Interprets and uses nonfiction text features such as maps, charts, tables, flow charts, diagrams, time lines | Decodes text using knowledge of common letter-sound correspondences, including blends, digraphs, consonant variants, r-controlled vowels, and a variety of spelling patterns | Decodes text using knowledge of the structure of words such as endings, prefixes, suffixes, compound words, contractions, and root words | Identifies variant sounds of consonants and vowels | Integrates meaning, structure, and visual cues to decode and comprehend text | Uses strategies of sampling, predicting, confirming, and self-correction independently | Makes inferences from texts | Reads longer, less-predictable texts with complex text structures | Identifies nonfiction text structures such as descriptive, problem/solution, time order, compare/contrast, cause/effect, and directions |
|---|---|---|---|---|---|---|---|---|---|---|
| | | | | | | | | | | |
| | | | | | | | | | | |
| | | | | | | | | | | |
| | | | | | | | | | | |
| | | | | | | | | | | |
| | | | | | | | | | | |

**Comments/Concerns**

_____

_____

_____

_____

_____

_____

# Word Awareness

Student _____

**Directions:** Say the sentence. Have the student repeat the sentence and tell you the number of words.
**Example:** *This is my dog. I can hear four words in this sentence.*

|  | **Pretest** Date _____ | **Posttest** Date _____ |
|---|---|---|
| I see my cat. | /4 | /4 |
| Can you do this? | /4 | /4 |
| This book is fun to read. | /6 | /6 |
| Please sit on the chair. | /5 | /5 |
| Where do you live? | /4 | /4 |
| **Score** | **/23** | **/23** |

Observations: _____

_____

# Syllable Awareness

Student _____

**Directions:** Say the word. Have the student repeat the word and clap for the number of syllables.
**Example:** Engine. *I hear two syllables in **engine**.*

|  | **Pretest** Date _____ | **Posttest** Date _____ |
|---|---|---|
| happy | /2 | /2 |
| Saturday | /3 | /3 |
| book | /1 | /1 |
| sunshine | /2 | /2 |
| experiment | /4 | /4 |
| **Score** | **/12** | **/12** |

Observations: _____

_____

# Listening for Rhyme

Student _____

**Directions:** Say the word pairs and ask the student if the words rhyme.
**Example:** Roast/toast. *Yes, these words rhyme.* Roast/ran. *No, these words don't rhyme.*

|  | Pretest Date _____ | Posttest Date _____ |
|---|---|---|
| bug/rug |  |  |
| pink/sink |  |  |
| big/box |  |  |
| hop/hip |  |  |
| jump/pump |  |  |
| **Score** | **/5** | **/5** |

Observations: _____

_____

**Directions:** Say the pair of words and ask the student if the words rhyme. If the student answers correctly, put a ✓. If the student's response is incorrect, put an **X**. **Example:** box/fox. *Yes.*

| must/dust *(yes)* |  | eat/feet *(yes)* |  |
|---|---|---|---|
| hope/joke *(no)* |  | pack/last *(no)* |  |
| kit/mitt *(yes)* |  | sent/bent *(yes)* |  |
|  |  | **Score** | **/6** |

Observations: _____

_____

**Directions:** Say the pair of words and ask the student if the words rhyme. If the student answers correctly, put a ✓. If the student's response is incorrect, put an **X**. **Example:** box/fox. *Yes.*

| cat/hat *(yes)* |  | leg/peg *(yes)* |  |
|---|---|---|---|
| man/let *(no)* |  | tab/top *(no)* |  |
| Sam/ram *(yes)* |  | hit/sit *(yes)* |  |
|  |  | **Score** | **/6** |

Observations: _____

_____

**Directions:** Say the pair of words and ask the student if the words rhyme. If the student answers correctly, put a ✓. If the student's response is incorrect, put an **X**. **Example:** box/fox. *Yes.*

| make/take *(yes)* |  | luck/stuck *(yes)* |  |
|---|---|---|---|
| fist/list *(yes)* |  | top/clip *(no)* |  |
| pen/jam *(no)* |  | file/style *(yes)* |  |
|  |  | **Score** | **/6** |

Observations: _____

_____

# Identifying Rhyme

Student _____

**Directions:** Say each set of words. Then have the student say the two words that rhyme. Put a ✔ if the student's response is correct. If not, record the words the student chooses.
**Example:** mat/hat/lid. *Mat, hat.*

| | |
|---|---|
| hog/fog/pen *(hog, fog)* | |
| lid/mad/rid *(lid, rid)* | |
| tap/let/sap *(tap, sap)* | |
| back/knock/sock *(knock, sock)* | |
| nod/net/bet *(net, bet)* | |
| fun/sun/den *(fun, sun)* | |
| **Score** | /6 |

Observations: _____

_____

**Directions:** Say each set of words. Then have the student say the two words that rhyme. Put a ✔ if the student's response is correct. If not, record the words the student chooses.
**Example:** mat/hat/lid. *Mat, hat.*

| | |
|---|---|
| lack/tack/sick *(lack, tack)* | |
| wig/jig/jag *(wig, jig)* | |
| gum/jam/sum *(gum, sum)* | |
| age/nudge/page *(age, page)* | |
| mind/mend/bend *(mend, bend)* | |
| hate/hoot/suit *(hoot, suit)* | |
| **Score** | /6 |

Observations: _____

_____

**Directions:** Say each set of words. Then have the student say the two words that rhyme. Put a ✔ if the student's response is correct. If not, record the words the student chooses. **Example:** mat/hat/lid. *Mat, hat.*

| | |
|---|---|
| cake/take/neck *(cake, take)* | |
| goat/get/boat *(goat, boat)* | |
| bell/call/sell *(bell, sell)* | |
| hood/good/head *(hood, good)* | |
| back/lick/sick *(lick/sick)* | |
| let/lot/spot *(lot, spot)* | |
| **Score** | /6 |

Observations: _____

_____

**Directions:** Say each set of words. Then have the student say the two words that rhyme. Put a ✔ if the student's response is correct. If not, record the words the student chooses. **Example:** mat/hat/lid. *Mat, hat.*

| | |
|---|---|
| bait/wait/sight *(bait, wait)* | |
| come/came/some *(come, some)* | |
| leg/tag/peg *(leg, peg)* | |
| meet/feet/rate *(meet, feet)* | |
| face/hiss/miss *(hiss, miss)* | |
| did/dude/rude *(dude, rude)* | |
| **Score** | /6 |

Observations: _____

_____

# Producing Rhyme

Student _____

**Directions:** Say the rhyming pair. Then ask the student to say another real or nonsense word that rhymes with the pair. Record the student's response.
**Example:** light/bite. *Kite.*

| | | | |
|---|---|---|---|
| lick/stick | | welt/pelt | |
| bought/caught | | must/trust | |
| lake/make | | ball/fall | |
| | | Score | /6 |

Observations: _____
_____

**Directions:** Say the rhyming pair. Then ask the student to say another real or nonsense word that rhymes with the pair. Record the student's response.
**Example:** light/bite. *Kite*

| | | | |
|---|---|---|---|
| snug/plug | | blame/frame | |
| trot/plot | | stole/pole | |
| sweep/sleep | | skip/ship | |
| | | Score | /6 |

Observations: _____
_____

**Directions:** Say the rhyming pair. Then ask the student to say another real or nonsense word that rhymes with the pair. Record the student's response.
**Example:** light/bite. *Kite.*

| | | | |
|---|---|---|---|
| skunk/trunk | | fret/set | |
| show/crow | | store/snore | |
| thrill/chill | | trash/smash | |
| | | Score | /6 |

Observations: _____
_____

**Directions:** Say the rhyming pair. Then ask the student to say another real or nonsense word that rhymes with the pair. Record the student's response.
**Example:** light/bite. *Kite.*

| | | | |
|---|---|---|---|
| place/case | | fluff/stuff | |
| check/speck | | missed/wrist | |
| oak/stroke | | please/bees | |
| | | Score | /6 |

Observations: _____
_____

# Listening for Initial Sounds

Student _____

**Directions:** Say the word. Have the student repeat the word and tell you the sound at the beginning. **Example:** Hat. /h/.

| | Pretest<br>Date _____ | Posttest<br>Date _____ |
|---|---|---|
| turtle | | |
| man | | |
| sink | | |
| pudding | | |
| leg | | |
| **Score** | /5 | /5 |

Observations: _____
_____

**Directions:** Say the word and ask the student to tell you the beginning sound. If the student answers correctly, put a ✓. If the student misses the sound, record the error. **Example:** sack. /s/.

| | | | |
|---|---|---|---|
| seed *(/s/)* | | meat *(/m/)* | |
| mark *(/m/)* | | medicine *(/m/)* | |
| save *(/s/)* | | second *(/s/)* | |
| | | **Score** | /6 |

Observations: _____
_____

**Directions:** Say the word and ask the student to tell you if the word begins with /m/. If the student answers correctly, put a ✓. If the student's response is incorrect, put an **X**. **Example:** moon. *Yes.*

| | | | |
|---|---|---|---|
| mittens *(yes)* | | tape *(no)* | |
| ball *(no)* | | mushroom *(yes)* | |
| mat *(yes)* | | mask *(yes)* | |
| | | **Score** | /6 |

Observations: _____
_____

**Directions:** Say the word and ask the student to tell you the beginning sound. If the student answers correctly, put a ✓. If the student misses the sound, record the error. **Example:** table. /t/.

| | | | |
|---|---|---|---|
| surprise *(/s/)* | | toy *(/t/)* | |
| talk *(/t/)* | | soft *(/s/)* | |
| mouth *(/m/)* | | tomorrow *(/t/)* | |
| | | **Score** | /6 |

Observations: _____
_____

# Listening for Final Sounds

Student _____

**Directions:** Say the word. Have the student repeat the word and tell you the sound at the end. **Example:** hat. *I hear* /t/ *at the end of the word* **hat**.

|  | Pretest Date _____ | Posttest Date _____ |
|---|---|---|
| park |  |  |
| noise |  |  |
| rabbit |  |  |
| trap |  |  |
| head |  |  |
| Score | /5 | /5 |

Observations: _____

_____

**Directions:** Say the word and ask the student to tell you the ending sound. If the student answers correctly, put a ✓. If the student misses the sound, record the error. **Example: she.** /ē/

| silo (/ō/) |  | polo (/ō/) |  |
|---|---|---|---|
| bee (/ē/) |  | tree (/ē/) |  |
| pro (/ō/) |  | echo (/ō/) |  |
| | | Score | /6 |

Observations: _____

_____

**Directions:** Say the word and ask the student to tell you the ending sound. If the student answers correctly, put a ✓. If the student misses the sound, record the error. **Example: brisk.** /sk/

| cost (/st/) |  | past (/st/) |  |
|---|---|---|---|
| wisp (/sp/) |  | crisp (/sp/) |  |
| disk (/sk/) |  | dusk (/sk/) |  |
| | | Score | /6 |

Observations: _____

**Directions:** Say the word and ask the student to tell you the ending sound. If the student answers correctly, put a ✓. If the student misses the sound, record the error. **Example: hat.** /t/

| bib (/b/) |  | night (/t/) |  |
|---|---|---|---|
| lap (/p/) |  | moss (/s/) |  |
| rain (/n/) |  | cram (/m/) |  |
| | | Score | /6 |

Observations: _____

_____

# Listening for Final Sounds

Student _____

**Directions:** Say the word and ask the student to tell you the ending sound. If the student answers correctly, put a ✓. If the student misses the sound, record the error. **Example:** hat. /t/

| | | | |
|---|---|---|---|
| clam *(/m/)* | | mine *(/n/)* | |
| quite *(/t/)* | | flap *(/p/)* | |
| fuss *(/s/)* | | fib *(/b/)* | |
| | | **Score** | /6 |

Observations: _____

_____

# Listening for Medial Sounds

**Directions:** Say the word. Have the student repeat the word and tell you the sound in the middle. **Example:** hat. *I hear /a/ in the middle of the word hat.*

| | Pretest Date _____ | Posttest Date _____ |
|---|---|---|
| pet | | |
| sack | | |
| hit | | |
| stop | | |
| cut | | |
| **Score** | /5 | /5 |

Observations: _____

_____

**Directions:** Say the word and ask the student to tell you if the middle sound in the word is /a/. If the student answers correctly, put a ✓. If the student's response is incorrect, put an **X**. **Example:** hat. *Yes.*

| | | | |
|---|---|---|---|
| sag *(yes)* | | pan *(yes)* | |
| bat *(yes)* | | lip *(no)* | |
| met *(no)* | | tap *(yes)* | |
| | | **Score** | /6 |

Observations: _____

_____

# Differentiating Initial Sounds

Student _____

**Directions:** Say the words. Have the student repeat the words and say which word starts with a different sound. **Example:** mix, man, nose. Nose *starts with a different sound.*

|  | Pretest Date _____ | Posttest Date _____ |
|---|---|---|
| bag, bug, cup |  |  |
| table, nut, tent |  |  |
| cup, cat, bat |  |  |
| fish, pan, pig |  |  |
| sun, sit, man |  |  |
| **Score** | **/5** | **/5** |

Observations: _____

_____

**Directions:** Say each set of words. Then have the student say the two words that begin with the same sound. Put a ✔ if the student's response is correct. If not, record the words the student chooses. **Example:** milk/toe/money. *milk, money.*

| | |
|---|---|
| face/factory/tunnel *(face, factory)* | |
| neck/singer/supper *(singer, supper)* | |
| nails/tennis/note *(nails, note)* | |
| many/farm/mud *(many, mud)* | |
| nurse/tank/Tuesday *(tank, Tuesday)* | |
| faucet/four/sausage *(faucet, four)* | |
| **Score** | **/6** |

Observations: _____

_____

**Directions:** Say each set of words. Then have the student say the two words that begin with the same sound. Put a ✔ if the student's response is correct. If not, record the words the student chooses. **Example:** milk/toe/money. *milk, money.*

| | |
|---|---|
| new/number/tall *(new, number)* | |
| today/north/tool *(today, tool)* | |
| teacher/south/soup *(south, soup)* | |
| many/monster/soft *(many, monster)* | |
| take/mother/tail *(take, tail)* | |
| minute/name/nap *(name, nap)* | |
| **Score** | **/6** |

Observations: _____

_____

**Directions:** Say each set of words. Then have the student say the two words that begin with the same sound. Put a ✔ if the student's response is correct. If not, record the words the student chooses. **Example:** milk/toe/money. *milk, money.*

| | |
|---|---|
| cabbage/cart/money *(cabbage, cart)* | |
| safety/pilot/salami *(safety, salami)* | |
| paint/family/pencil *(paint, pencil)* | |
| full/field/noise *(full, field)* | |
| cotton/tadpole/taxi *(tadpole, taxi)* | |
| piano/cane/cushion *(cane, cushion)* | |
| **Score** | **/6** |

Observations: _____

_____

# Differentiating Final Sounds

Student _____

**Directions:** Say each set of words. Then have the student say the two words that end with the same sound. Put a ✓ if the student's response is correct. If not, record the words the student chooses. **Example:** wing/long/sink. *wing, long.*

| | |
|---|---|
| and/dent/pond *(and, pond)* | |
| bend/land/ant *(bend, land)* | |
| wrong/blink/drank *(blink, drank)* | |
| honk/song/think *(honk, think)* | |
| plant/front/bang *(plant, front)* | |
| bunk/bent/plant *(bent, plant)* | |
| **Score** | **/6** |

Observations: _____

_____

**Directions:** Say each set of words. Then have the student say the two words that end with the same sound. Put a ✓ if the student's response is correct. If not, record the words the student chooses. **Example:** dig/peg/mad. *dig, peg.*

| | | |
|---|---|---|
| pan/fin/pop *(pan, fin)* | | log/nod/wig *(log, wig)* |
| led/leg/did *(led, did)* | | rib/top/dip *(top, dip)* |
| got/pal/fall *(pal, fall)* | | wet/mitt/miss *(wet, mitt)* |
| | **Score** | **/6** |

Observations: _____

_____

**Directions:** Say each set of words. Then have the student say the two words that end with the same sound. Put a ✓ if the student's response is correct. If not, record the words the student chooses. **Example:** rich/such/dish. *rich, such.*

| | |
|---|---|
| blush/beach/push *(blush, push)* | |
| peach/rush/pouch *(peach, pouch)* | |
| mash/coach/grouch *(coach, grouch)* | |
| rich/dash/fish *(dash, fish)* | |
| crush/trash/inch *(crush, trash)* | |
| teach/such/smash *(teach, such)* | |
| **Score** | **/6** |

Observations: _____

_____

# Differentiating Medial Sounds

**Directions:** Say the word and ask the student to tell you the middle sound. If the student answers correctly, put a ✓. If the student misses the sound, record the error. **Example:** hat. /a/

| | | |
|---|---|---|
| knot *(/ô/)* | | snack *(/a/)* |
| cliff *(/i/)* | | plop *(/ô/)* |
| dock *(/ô/)* | | quit *(/i/)* |
| | **Score** | **/6** |

Observations: _____

_____

Foundational Skills Assessments

# Differentiating Medial Sounds

Student _____

**Directions:** Say the pair of words and ask the student if the words have the same middle sound. If the student answers correctly, put a ✓. If the student misses the sound, record the error. **Example:** frame/race. *yes.*

| | |
|---|---|
| shave/blade *(yes)* | grace/mist *(no)* |
| trace/track *(no)* | wake/plate *(yes)* |
| grade/vane *(yes)* | fad/fade *(no)* |
| | Score /6 |

Observations: _____

_____

**Directions:** Say each set of words and have the student say the two words that have the same middle sound. If the student answers correctly, put a ✓. If the student misses the sound, record the error. **Example:** bar/lark/stack. *bar, lark.*

| | |
|---|---|
| charge/dodge/dart *(charge, dart)* | |
| prop/barge/tarp *(barge, tarp)* | |
| match/harp/char *(harp, char)* | |
| lard/land/large *(lard, large)* | |
| tar/yarn/been *(tar, yarn)* | |
| chart/carp/cap *(chart, carp)* | |
| Score | /6 |

Observations: _____

_____

**Directions:** Say the pair of words and ask the student if the words have the same middle sound. If the student answers correctly, put a ✓. If the student misses the sound, record the error. **Example:** trail/sail. *yes.*

| | |
|---|---|
| vain/raise *(yes)* | praise/grant *(no)* |
| stack/paid *(no)* | quaint/fail *(yes)* |
| quail/sprain *(yes)* | land/grain *(no)* |
| | Score /6 |

Observations: _____

_____

**Directions:** Say the pair of words and ask the student if the words have the same middle sound. If the student answers correctly, put a ✓. If the student misses the sound, record the error. **Example:** trail/sail. *yes.*

| | |
|---|---|
| rinse/mist *(yes)* | sit/sat *(no)* |
| smack/gift *(no)* | slip/crib *(yes)* |
| pack/snap *(yes)* | fax/fix *(no)* |
| | Score /6 |

Observations: _____

_____

# Differentiating Initial, Final, and Medial Sounds

Student _____

**Directions:** Say the words. Have the student say the words and tell you which sound is the same in the words. **Example:** Boy, toy, soil. *I hear /oi/ in all three words.*

| | Pretest<br>Date _____ | Posttest<br>Date _____ |
|---|---|---|
| damp, romp, lump (/mp/) | | |
| make, train, tray (/ /) | | |
| saw, hawk, ball (/ô/) | | |
| small, smiling, smack (/sm/) | | |
| rest, waist, stick (/st/) | | |
| fish, shake, stash (/sh/) | | |
| corn, chore, roar (/ôr/) | | |
| stove, cold, goat (/ /) | | |
| hand, lend, bland (/nd/) | | |
| such, bench, church (/ch/) | | |
| spoon, chew, blue (/o͞o/) | | |
| wheat, whistle, whisper (/wh/) | | |
| **Score** | /12 | /12 |

Observations: _____

_____

*Foundational Skills Assessments*

# Blending Onset and Rime

Student _____

**Directions:** Say the first sound of the word followed by the rest of the word. Then have the student say the whole word. If the student says the word correctly, put a ✓. If the student misses the word, record the error. **Example:** /b/ /at/. *bat.*

| | | | |
|---|---|---|---|
| /p/ /in/ (pin) | | /n/ /ap/ (nap) | |
| /m/ /at/ (mat) | | /p/ /it/ (pit) | |
| /s/ /it/ (sit) | | /m/ /an/ (man) | |
| | | Score | /6 |

Observations: _____

_____

**Directions:** Say the first sound of the word followed by the rest of the word. Then have the student say the whole word. If the student says the word correctly, put a ✓. If the student misses the word, record the error. **Example:** /b/ /at/. *bat.*

| | | | |
|---|---|---|---|
| /l/ /ick/ (lik) | | /l/ /ess/ (les) | |
| /d/ /uck/ (duk) | | /b/ /ud/ (bud) | |
| /f/ /an/ (fan) | | /f/ /og/ (fog) | |
| | | Score | /6 |

Observations: _____

_____

**Directions:** Say the first sound of the word followed by the rest of the word. Then have the student say the whole word. If the student says the word correctly, put a ✓. If the student misses the word, record the error. **Example:** /b/ /at/. *bat.*

| | | | |
|---|---|---|---|
| /b/ /us/ (bus) | | /m/ /ill/ (mil) | |
| /h/ /ot/ (hot) | | /t/ /uck/ (tuk) | |
| /f/ /un/ (fun) | | /s/ /ad/ (sad) | |
| | | Score | /6 |

Observations: _____

_____

**Directions:** Say the first sound of the word followed by the rest of the word. Then have the student say the whole word. If the student says the word correctly, put a ✓. If the student misses the word, record the error. **Example:** /b/ /at/. *bat.*

| | | | |
|---|---|---|---|
| /g/ /as/ (gas) | | /s/ /ip/ (sip) | |
| /b/ /eg/ (beg) | | /d/ /eck/ (dek) | |
| /c/ /ut/ (cut) | | /g/ /ab/ (gab) | |
| | | Score | /6 |

Observations: _____

_____

# Segmenting Onset and Rime

Student _____

**Directions:** Say the word. Have the student repeat the word, say the first sound in the word, and then say the rest of the word. **Example:** fig: /f/ /ig/ *fig*.

| | Pretest Date _____ | Posttest Date _____ |
|---|---|---|
| cat: /k/ /at/ | | |
| run: /r/ /un/ | | |
| pop: /p/ /op/ | | |
| hen: /h/ /en/ | | |
| rid: /r/ /id/ | | |
| **Score** | /5 | /5 |

Observations: _____

_____

**Directions:** Say the word. Have the student say the first sound followed by the rest of the word and then say the whole word. If the student segments the word correctly, put a ✔. If the student's response is incorrect, record the error. **Example:** bat. /b/ /at/, *bat*.

| | | | |
|---|---|---|---|
| got (*/g/ /ot/, got*) | | dot (*/d/ /ot/, dot*) | |
| well (*/w/ /ell/, well*) | | wag (*/w/ /ag/, wag*) | |
| pad (*/p/ /ad/, pad*) | | fed (*/f/ /ed/, fed*) | |
| | | **Score** | /6 |

Observations: _____

_____

**Directions:** Say the word. Have the student say the first sound followed by the rest of the word and then say the whole word. If the student segments the word correctly, put a ✔. If the student's response is incorrect, record the error. **Example:** bat. /b/ /at/, *bat*.

| | | | |
|---|---|---|---|
| hot (*/h/ /ot/, hot*) | | pop (*/p/ /op/, pop*) | |
| win (*/w/ /in/, win*) | | hill (*/h/ /ill/, hill*) | |
| tap (*/t/ /ap/, tap*) | | lack (*/l/ /ak/, lack*) | |
| | | **Score** | /6 |

Observations: _____

_____

**Directions:** Say the word. Have the student say the first sound followed by the rest of the word and then say the whole word. If the student segments the word correctly, put a ✔. If the student's response is incorrect, record the error. **Example:** bat. /b/ /at/, *bat*.

| | | | |
|---|---|---|---|
| doll (*/d/ /oll/, dol*) | | cup (*/c/ /up/, cup*) | |
| jet (*/j/ /et/, jet*) | | miss (*/m/ /is/, miss*) | |
| pat (*/p/ /at/, pat*) | | neck (*/n/ /ek/, neck*) | |
| | | **Score** | /6 |

Observations: _____

_____

Foundational Skills Assessments

# Segmenting Phonemes

Student _____

**Directions:** Say the word. Have the student tell you all the sounds in the word.
**Example:** If I say run, you will say /r/ /u/ /n/.

| | Pretest Date | Posttest Date |
|---|---|---|
| cat: /k/ /a/ /t/ | /3 | /3 |
| top: /t/ /ô/ p/ | /3 | /3 |
| said: /s/ /e/ /d/ | /3 | /3 |
| jumps: /j/ /u/ /m/ /p/ /s/ | /5 | /5 |
| rugs: /r/ /u/ /g/ /z/ | /4 | /4 |
| **Score** | /18 | /18 |

Observations: _____
_____

**Directions:** Say the word. Have the student say the word sound by sound and then say the whole word. If the student segments the word correctly, put a ✓. If the student's response is incorrect, record the error. **Example:** sip. /s/ /i/ /p/, *sip.*

| | | | |
|---|---|---|---|
| yet (/y/ /e/ /t/, yet) | | him (/h/ /i/ /m/, him) | |
| bun (/b/ /u/ /n/, bun) | | yell (/y/ /e/ /ll/, yell) | |
| peg (/p/ /e/ /g/, peg) | | lip (/ll/ /i/ /p/, lip) | |
| | | **Score** | /6 |

Observations: _____
_____

**Directions:** Say the word. Have the student say the word sound by sound and then say the whole word. If the student segments the word correctly, put a ✓. If the student's response is incorrect, record the error. **Example:** sip. /s/ /i/ /p/, *sip.*

| | | | |
|---|---|---|---|
| jig (/j/ /i/ /g/, jig) | | den (/d/ /e/ /n/, den) | |
| rub (/r/ /u/ /b/, rub) | | bag (/b/ /a/ /g/, bag) | |
| pep (/p/ /e/ /p/, pep) | | pod (/p/ /o/ /d/, pod) | |
| | | **Score** | /6 |

Observations: _____
_____

**Directions:** Say the word. Have the student say the word sound by sound and then say the whole word. If the student segments the word correctly, put a ✓. If the student's response is incorrect, record the error. **Example:** sip. /s/ /i/ /p/, *sip.*

| | | | |
|---|---|---|---|
| well (/w/ /e/ /ll/, well) | | quack (/kw/ /a/ /k/, quack) | |
| cup (/k/ /u/ /p/, cup) | | get (/g/ /e/ /t/, get) | |
| knob (/n/ /ô/ /b/, knob) | | hip (/h/ /i/ /p/, hip) | |
| | | **Score** | /6 |

Observations: _____
_____

# Blending Phonemes

Student _____

**Directions:** Say the word sound by sound. Then have the student say the word. **Example:** *I will say the sounds of some words. I want you to blend the sounds and say the word.* **Example:** /r/ /u/ /t/: rut.

|  | Pretest Date | Posttest Date |
|---|---|---|
| /n/ /u/ /t/: nut | | |
| /j/ /e/ /t/: jet | | |
| /w/ /i/ /g/: wig | | |
| /s/ /a/ /t/: sat | | |
| /m/ /ô/ /p/: mop | | |
| **Score** | **/5** | **/5** |

Observations: _____

_____

**Directions:** Say the word sound by sound. Then have the student say the word. Put a ✔ if the student's response is correct. If the student misses the word, record the error. **Example:** /sh/ /o͞o/. *shoe.*

| /pr/ /o͞o/ /f/ (proof) | |
|---|---|
| /sn/ /o͞o/ /p/ (snoop) | |
| /gl/ /o͞o/ (glue) | |
| /bl/ /o͞o/ (blew) | |
| /pl/ /o͞o/ /m/ (plume) | |
| /sm/ /o͞o/ /th/ (smooth) | |
| **Score** | **/6** |

Observations: _____

_____

**Directions:** Say the word sound by sound. Then have the student say the word. **Example:** *I will say the sounds of some words. I want you to blend the sounds and say the words: for example,* /s/ /p/ /oi/ /l/ : spoil.

|  | Pretest Date | Posttest Date |
|---|---|---|
| /r/ /e/ /n/ /ch/: wrench | | |
| /k/ /o͝o/ /d/: could | | |
| /g/ /r/ /a/ /n/ /d/: grand | | |
| /s/ /t/ /o͞o/ /d/: stood | | |
| /s/ /l/ /ur/ /p/: slurp | | |
| /t/ /r/ / / /t/: treat | | |
| /h/ /a/ /p/ / /: happy | | |
| /th/ /ôr/ /n/: thorn | | |
| /w/ /ô/ /k/: walk | | |
| /ch/ /a/ /m/ /p/: champ | | |
| /r/ /ou/ /n/ /d/: round | | |
| /s/ /t/ /r/ / / /k/: stroke | | |
| **Score** | **/12** | **/12** |

Observations: _____

_____

**Directions:** Say the word sound by sound. Then have the student say the word. Put a ✔ if the student's response is correct. If the student misses the word, record the error. **Example:** /str/ /u/ /m/. *strum*

| /skr/ / / /p/ (scrape) | |
|---|---|
| /spl/ /ī/ /s/ (splice) | |
| /spr/ /e/ /d/ (spread) | |
| /str/ /i/ /ng/ (string) | |
| /skw/ / / /k/ (squeak) | |
| /skw/ /ô/ /d/ (squad) | |
| **Score** | **/6** |

Observations: _____

_____

Foundational Skills Assessments

©2017 Benchmark Education Company, LLC

# Blending Phonemes

Student _____

**Directions:** Say the word sound by sound. Then have the student say the word. Put a ✓ if the student's response is correct. If the student misses the word, record the error.**Example:** /d/ /o/ /g/. *dog.*

| | | |
|---|---|---|
| /d/ /u/ /g/ (dug) | /s/ /a/ /p/ (sap) | |
| /m/ /e/ /t/ (met) | /k/ /ô/ /b/ (cob) | |
| /p/ /i/ /n/ (pin) | /d/ /e/ /n/ (den) | |
| | **Score** | /6 |

Observations: _____

_____

**Directions:** Say the word sound by sound. Then have the student say the word. Put a ✓ if the student's response is correct. If the student misses the word, record the error.**Example:** /d/ /o/ /g/. *dog.*

| | | |
|---|---|---|
| /v/ /a/ /n/ (van) | /h/ /i/ /l/ (hill) | |
| /b/ /u/ /s/ (bus) | /j/ /e/ /t/ (jet) | |
| /w/ /e/ /b/ (web) | /m/ /ô/ /s/ (moss) | |
| | **Score** | /6 |

Observations: _____

_____

**Directions:** Say the word sound by sound. Then have the student say the word. Put a ✓ if the student's response is correct. If the student misses the word, record the error. **Example:** /d/ /o/ /g/. *dog.*

| | | |
|---|---|---|
| /p/ /ô/ /d/ (pod) | /p/ /u/ /f/ (puff) | |
| /r/ /a/ /p/ (rap) | /d/ /i/ /d/ (did) | |
| /w/ /i/ /g/ (wig) | /w/ /e/ /t/ (wet) | |
| | **Score** | /6 |

Observations: _____

_____

**Directions:** Say the word sound by sound. Then have the student say the word. Put a ✓ if the student's response is correct. If the student misses the word, record the error. **Example:** /d/ /o/ /g/. *dog.*

| | | |
|---|---|---|
| /t/ /a/ /ks/ (tax) | /t/ /a/ /b/ (tab) | |
| /s/ /u/ /n/ (sun) | /m/ /i/ /ks/ (mix) | |
| /f/ /e/ /l/ (fell) | /t/ /ô/ /t/ (tot) | |
| | **Score** | /6 |

Observations: _____

_____

# Substituting Initial Sounds

Student _____

**Directions:** Say the word, and then segment it sound by sound. Ask the student to replace the first sound in the word with the new sound while segmenting sound by sound and then say the new word. Put a ✔ if the student's response is correct. If the student misses the word, record the error. **Example:** spell, /sp/ /e/ /l/. Change /sp/ to /sm/. /sm/ /e/ /l/, smell.

| | | | |
|---|---|---|---|
| span, /sp/ /a/ /n/<br>Change /sp/ to /sk/.<br>*(/sk/ /a/ /n/, scan)* | | smack, /sm/ /a/ /k/<br>Change /sm/ to /st/.<br>*(/st/ /a/ /k/, stack)* | |
| snake, /sn/ / / /k/<br>Change /sn/ to /st/.<br>*(/st/ /a/ /k/, stake)* | | swim, /sw/ /i/ /m/<br>Change /sw/ to /sl/.<br>*(/sl/ /i/ /m/, slim)* | |
| skip, /sk/ /i/ /p/<br>Change /sk/ to /sn/.<br>*(/sn/ /i/ /p/, snip)* | | skin, /sk/ /i/ /n/<br>Change /sk/ to /sp/.<br>*(/sp/ /i/ /n/, spin)* | |
| | | **Score** | /6 |

Observations: _____

_____

**Directions:** Say the word, and then segment it sound by sound. Ask the student to replace the first sound in the word with the new sound while segmenting sound by sound and then say the new word. Put a ✔ if the student's response is correct. If the student misses the word, record the error. **Example:** jam, /j/ /a/ /m/. Change /j/ to /l/. /l/ /a/ /m/, lamb.

| | | | |
|---|---|---|---|
| strong, /str/ /ô/ /ng/<br>Change /str/ to /r/.<br>*(/r/ /ô/ /ng/, wrong)* | | slime, /sl/ /ī/ /m/<br>Change /sl/ to /r/.<br>*(/r/ /ī/ /m/, rhyme)* | |
| calf, /k/ /a/ /f/<br>Change /k/ to /h/.<br>*(/h/ /a/ /f/, half)* | | crumb, /kr/ /u/ /m/<br>Change /kr/ to /th/.<br>*(/th/ /u/ /m/, thumb)* | |
| crow, /kr/ / /<br>Change /kr/ to /n/.<br>*(/n/ / /, know)* | | flat, /fl/ /a/ /t/<br>Change /fl/ to /n/.<br>*(/n/ /a/ /t/, gnat)* | |
| | | **Score** | /6 |

Observations: _____

_____

**Directions:** Say the word, and then segment it sound by sound. Ask the student to replace the first sound in the word with the new sound while segmenting sound by sound and then say the new word. Put a ✔ if the student's response is correct. If the student misses the word, record the error. **Example:** fat, /f/ /a/ /t/. Change /f/ to /th/. /th/ /a/ /t/, that.

| | | | |
|---|---|---|---|
| tale, /t/ / / /l/<br>Change /t/ to /wh/.<br>*(/wh/ / / /l/, whale)* | | sniff, /sn/ /i/ /f/<br>Change /sn/ to /wh/.<br>*(/wh/ /i/ /f/, whiff)* | |
| cloth, /kl/ /o/ /th/<br>Change /kl/ to /sl/.<br>*(/sl/ /o/ /th/, sloth)* | | slick, /sl/ /i/ /k/<br>Change /sl/ to /th/.<br>*(/th/ /i/ /k/, thick)* | |
| pink, /p/ /i/ /nk/<br>Change /p/ to /th/.<br>*(/th/ /i/ /nk/, think)* | | spite, /sp/ /ī/ /t/<br>Change /sp/ to /wh/.<br>*(/wh/ /ī/ /t/, white)* | |
| | | **Score** | /6 |

Observations: _____

_____

**Directions:** Say the word, and then segment it sound by sound. Ask the student to replace the first sound in the word with the new sound while segmenting sound by sound and then say the new word. Put a ✔ if the student's response is correct. If the student misses the word, record the error. **Example:** fork, /f/ /ôr/ /k/. Change /f/ to /st/. /st/ /ôr/ /k/, stork.

| | | | |
|---|---|---|---|
| port, /p/ /ôr/ /t/<br>Change /p/ to /sn/.<br>*(/sn/ /ôr/ /t/, snort)* | | poor, /p/ /ôr/<br>Change /p/ to /fl/.<br>*(/fl/ /ôr/, floor)* | |
| roar, /r/ /ôr/<br>Change initial /r/ to /s/.<br>*(/s/ /ôr/, soar)* | | thorn, /th/ /ôr/ /n/<br>Change /th/ to /sk/.<br>*(/sk/ /ôr/ /n/, scorn)* | |
| porch, /p/ /ôr/ /ch/<br>Change /p/ to /t/.<br>*(/t/ /ôr/ /ch/, torch)* | | tore, /t/ /ôr/<br>Change /t/ to /sn/.<br>*(/sn/ /ôr/, snore)* | |
| | | **Score** | /6 |

Observations: _____

_____

# Substituting Medial Sounds

Student _____

**Directions:** Say the word, and then segment it sound by sound. Ask the student to replace the middle sound in the word with the new sound while segmenting sound by sound and then say the new word. Put a ✔ if the student's response is correct. If the student misses the word, record the error. **Example:** ride, /r/ / / /d/. Change / / to / /. /r/ / / /d/, rode.

| | | | |
|---|---|---|---|
| cave, /c/ / / /v/<br>Change / / to / /.<br>*(/c/ / / /v/, cove)* | | line, /l/ /ī/ /n/<br>Change / / to / /.<br>*(/l/ / / /n/, lone)* | |
| can, /c/ /a/ /n/<br>Change /a/ to / /.<br>*(/c/ / / /n/, cone)* | | wave, /w/ / / /v/<br>Change / / to / /.<br>*(/w/ / / /v/, wove)* | |
| vat, /v/ /a/ /t/<br>Change /a/ to / /.<br>*(/v/ / / /t/, vote)* | | quit, /kw/ /i/ /t/<br>Change /i/ to / /.<br>*(/kw/ / / /t/, quote)* | |
| | | **Score** | /6 |

Observations: _____

_____

**Directions:** Say the word, and then segment it sound by sound. Ask the student to replace the middle sound in the word with the new sound while segmenting sound by sound and then say the new word. Put a ✔ if the student's response is correct. If the student misses the word, record the error. **Example:** cram, /kr/ /a/ /m/. Change /a/ to / /. /kr/ / / /m/, cream.

| | | | |
|---|---|---|---|
| strike, /str/ / / /k/<br>Change / / to / /.<br>*(/str/ / / /k/, streak)* | | slap, /sl/ /a/ /p/<br>Change /a/ to / /.<br>*(/sl/ / / /p/, sleep)* | |
| fried, /fr/ / / /d/<br>Change / / to / /.<br>*(/fr/ / / /d/, freed)* | | white, /wh/ / / /t/<br>Change / / to / /.<br>*(/wh/ / / /t/, wheat)* | |
| speck, /sp/ /e/ /k/<br>Change /e/ to / /.<br>*(/sp/ / / /k/, speak)* | | crock, /kr/ /ô/ /k/<br>Change /ô/ to / /.<br>*(/kr/ / / /k/, creek)* | |
| | | **Score** | /6 |

Observations: _____

_____

**Directions:** Say the word, and then segment it sound by sound. Ask the student to replace the middle sound in the word with the new sound while segmenting sound by sound and then say the new word. Put a ✔ if the student's response is correct. If the student misses the word, record the error. **Example:** wade, /w/ / / /d/. Change / / to / /. /w/ / / /d/, wide

| | | | |
|---|---|---|---|
| lake, /l/ / / /k/<br>Change / / to / /.<br>*(/l/ / / /k/, like)* | | grape, /gr/ / / /p/<br>Change / / to / /.<br>*(/gr/ / / /p/, gripe)* | |
| grim, /gr/ /i/ /m/<br>Change /i/ to / /.<br>*(/gr/ / / /m/, grime)* | | miss, /m/ /i/ /s/<br>Change /i/ to / /.<br>*(/m/ / / /s/, mice)* | |
| dome, /d/ / / /m/<br>Change / / to / /.<br>*(/d/ / / /m/, dime)* | | drove, /dr/ / / /v/<br>Change / / to / /.<br>*(/dr/ / / /v/, drive)* | |
| | | **Score** | /6 |

Observations: _____

_____

**Directions:** Say the word, and then segment it sound by sound. Ask the student to replace the middle sound in the word with the new sound while segmenting sound by sound and then say the new word. Put a ✔ if the student's response is correct. If the student misses the word, record the error. **Example:** bin, /b/ /i/ /n/. Change /i/ to /ûr/. /b/ /ûr/ /n/, burn.

| | | | |
|---|---|---|---|
| chain, /ch/ / / /n/<br>Change / / to /ûr/.<br>*(/ch/ /ûr/ /n/, churn)* | | time, /t/ /ī/ /m/<br>Change /ī/ to /ûr/.<br>*(/t/ /ûr/ /m/, term)* | |
| joke, /j/ / / /k/<br>Change / / to /ûr/.<br>*(/j/ /ûr/ /k/, jerk)* | | nice, /n/ /ī/ /s/<br>Change /ī/ to /ûr/.<br>*(/n/ /ûr/ /s/, nurse)* | |
| skate, /sk/ / / /t/<br>Change / / to /ûr/.<br>*(/sk/ /ûr/ /t/, skirt)* | | thud, /th/ /u/ /d/<br>Change /u/ to /ûr/.<br>*(/th/ /ûr/ /d/, third)* | |
| | | **Score** | /6 |

Observations: _____

_____

# Medial Sound Substitution

Student _____

**Directions:** Say the word, and then segment it sound by sound. Ask the student to replace the middle sound in the word with the new sound while segmenting sound by sound and then say the new word. Put a ✔ if the student's response is correct. If the student misses the word, record the error. **Example:** fight, /f/ /ī / /t/. Change /ī/ to oo /. /f/ /oo / /t/, foot.

| | | | |
|---|---|---|---|
| shade, /sh/ / / /d/ Change / / to /oo /. *(/sh/ /oo / /d/, should)* | | bash, /b/ /a/ /sh/ Change /a/ to /oo /. *(/b/ /oo / /sh/, bush)* | |
| hide, /h/ / / /d/ Change / / to /oo /. *(/h/ /oo / /d/, hood)* | | tile, /t/ /ī/ /l/ Change /ī/ to /oo /. *(/t/ /oo / /l/, tool)* | |
| brick, /br/ /i/ /k/ Change /i/ to /oo /. *(/br/ /oo / /k/, brook)* | | weed, /w/ / / /d/ Change / / to /oo /. *(/w/ /oo / /d/, would)* | |
| | | **Score** | /6 |

Observations: _____

_____

**Directions:** Say the word, and then segment it sound by sound. Ask the student to replace the middle sound in the word with the new sound while segmenting sound by sound and then say the new word. Put a ✔ if the student's response is correct. If the student misses the word, record the error. **Example:** sale, /s/ / / /l/. Change / / to /oi/. /s/ /oi/ /l/, soil.

| | | | |
|---|---|---|---|
| chase, /ch/ / / /s/ Change / / to /oi/. *(/ch/ /oi/ /s/, choice)* | | tea, /t/ / / Change / / to /oi/. *(/t/ /oi/, toy)* | |
| bay, /b/ / / Change /a/ to /oi/. *(/b/ /oi/, boy)* | | host, /h/ / / /st/ Change / / to /oi/. *(/h/ /oi/ /st/, hoist)* | |
| pant, /p/ /a/ /nt/ Change /a/ to /oi/. *(/p/ /oi/ /nt/, point)* | | play, /pl/ / / Change / / to /oi/. *(/pl/ /oi/, ploy)* | |
| | | **Score** | /6 |

Observations: _____

_____

**Directions:** Say the word, and then segment it sound by sound. Ask the student to replace the middle sound in the word with the new sound while segmenting sound by sound and then say the new word. Put a ✔ if the student's response is correct. If the student misses the word, record the error. **Example:** catch, /k/ /a/ /ch/. Change /a/ to /ou/. /k/ /ou/ /ch/, couch.

| | | | |
|---|---|---|---|
| fail, /f/ / / /l/ Change / / to /ou/. *(/f/ /ou/ /l/, fowl)* | | spite, /sp/ /ī/ /t/ Change /ī/ to /ou/. *(/sp/ /ou/ /t/, spout)* | |
| mind, /m/ /ī/ /nd/ Change /ī/ to /ou/. *(/m/ /ou/ /nd/, mound)* | | say, /s/ / / Change / / to /ou/. *(/s/ /ou/, sow)* | |
| scale, /sk/ / / /l/ Change / / to /ou/. *(/sk/ /ou/ /l/, scowl)* | | pride, /pr/ /ī/ /d/ Change /ī/ to /ou/. *(/pr/ /ou/ /d/, proud)* | |
| | | **Score** | /6 |

Observations: _____

_____

**Directions:** Say the word, and then segment it sound by sound. Ask the student to replace the middle sound in the word with the new sound while segmenting sound by sound and then say the new word. Put a ✔ if the student's response is correct. If the student misses the word, record the error. **Example:** man, /m/ /a/ /n/. Change /a/ to /e/. /m/ /e/ /n/, men

| | |
|---|---|
| tin, /t/ /i/ /n/ Change /i/ to /a/. *(/t/ /a/ /n/, tan)* | |
| big, /b/ /i/ /g/ Change /i/ to /e/. *(/b/ /e/ /g/, beg)* | |
| not, /n/ /ô/ /t/ Change /ô/ to /e/. *(/n/ /e/ /t/, net)* | |
| lock, /l/ /ô/ /k/ Change /ô/ to /u/. *(/l/ /u/ /k/, luck)* | |
| hem, /h/ /e/ /m/ Change /e/ to /a/. *(/h/ /a/ /m/, ham)* | |
| cub, /k/ /u/ /b/ Change /u/ to /ô/. *(/k/ /ô/ /b/, cob)* | |
| **Score** | /6 |

Observations: _____

_____

Foundational Skills Assessments                    ©2017 Benchmark Education Company, LLC

# Substituting Final Sounds

Student _____

**Directions:** Say the word, and then segment it sound by sound. Ask the student to replace the last sound in the word with the new sound while segmenting sound by sound and then say the new word. Put a ✓ if the student's response is correct. If the student misses the word, record the error. **Example:** bus, /b/ /u/ /s/. Change /s/ to /mp/. /b/ /u/ /mp/, bump.

| | | | |
|---|---|---|---|
| soap, /s/ /ō/ /p/<br>Change /p/ to /ft/.<br>*(/s/ /ō/ /ft/, soft)* | | fed, /f/ /e/ /d/<br>Change /d/ to /lt/.<br>*(/f/ /e/ /lt/, felt)* | |
| hem, /h/ /e/ /m/<br>Change /m/ to /lp/.<br>*(/h/ /e/ /lp/, help)* | | lost, /l/ /ô/ /st/<br>Change /st/ to /ft/.<br>*(/l/ /ô/ /ft/, loft)* | |
| slug, /sl/ /u/ /g/<br>Change /g/ to /mp/.<br>*(/sl/ /u/ /mp/, slump)* | | wind, /w/ /i/ /nd/<br>Change /nd/ to /lt/.<br>*(/w/ /i/ /lt/, wilt)* | |
| | | **Score** | /6 |

Observations: _____

_____

**Directions:** Say the word, and then segment it sound by sound. Ask the student to replace the last sound in the word with the new sound while segmenting sound by sound and then say the new word. Put a ✓ if the student's response is correct. If the student misses the word, record the error. **Example:** hay, /h/ /ā/. Change / / to / r/. /h/ / r/, hear

| | | | |
|---|---|---|---|
| no, /n/ / /<br>Change / / to / r/.<br>*(/n/ / r/, near)* | | pore, /p/ /ôr/<br>Change /ôr/ to / r/.<br>*(/p/ / r/, peer)* | |
| chore, /ch/ /ôr/<br>Change /ôr/ to / r/.<br>*(/ch/ / r/, cheer)* | | doe, /d/ /ō/<br>Change /ō/ to / r/.<br>*(/d/ / r/, dear)* | |
| clay, /kl/ /ā/<br>Change /ā/ to / r/.<br>*(/kl/ / r/, clear)* | | sty, /st/ / /<br>Change / / to / r/.<br>*(/st/ / r/, steer)* | |
| | | **Score** | /6 |

Observations: _____

_____

**Directions:** Say the word, and then segment it sound by sound. Ask the student to replace the last sound in the word with the new sound while segmenting sound by sound and then say the new word. Put a ✓ if the student's response is correct. If the student misses the word, record the error. **Example:** plum, /pl/ /u/ /m/. Change /m/ to /k/. /pl/ /u/ /k/, pluck.

| | | | |
|---|---|---|---|
| pet, /p/ /e/ /t/<br>Change /t/ to /k/.<br>*(/p/ /e/ /k/, peck)* | | crank, /kr/ /a/ /nk/<br>Change /nk/ to /k/.<br>*(/kr/ /a/ /k/, crack)* | |
| blast, /bl/ /a/ /st/<br>Change /st/ to /k/.<br>*(/bl/ /a/ /k/, black)* | | trip, /tr/ /i/ /p/<br>Change /p/ to /k/.<br>*(/tr/ /i/ /k/, trick)* | |
| strum, /str/ /u/ /m/<br>Change /m/ to /k/.<br>*(/str/ /u/ /k/, struck)* | | stamp, /st/ /a/ /mp/<br>Change /mp/ to /k/.<br>*(/st/ /a/ /k/, stack)* | |
| | | **Score** | /6 |

Observations: _____

_____

**Directions:** Say the word, and then segment it sound by sound. Ask the student to replace the last sound in the word with the new sound while segmenting sound by sound and then say the new word. Put a ✓ if the student's response is correct. If the student misses the word, record the error. **Example:** fan, /f/ /a/ /n/. Change /n/ to /âr/. /f/ /âr/, fair.

| | | | |
|---|---|---|---|
| flow, /fl/ /ō/<br>Change /ō/ to / r/.<br>*(/fl/ / r/, flare)* | | stay, /st/ / /<br>Change / / to / r/.<br>*(/st/ / r/, stare)* | |
| woe, /w/ /ō/<br>Change /ō/ to / r/.<br>*(/w/ / r/, wear)* | | pie, /p/ / /<br>Change / / to / r/.<br>*(/p/ / r/, pear)* | |
| high, /h/ / /<br>Change / / to / r/.<br>*(/h/ / r/, hair)* | | spy, /sp/ / /<br>Change / / to / r/.<br>*(/sp/ / r/, spare)* | |
| | | **Score** | /6 |

Observations: _____

_____

# Substituting Sounds

Student _____

**Directions:** Say the word. Ask the student to replace one of the sounds in the word with a new sound to create a new word. **Example:** *I can change the /sk/ in* **skate** *to /l/ to make the word* **late.**

| | Pretest<br>Date | Posttest<br>Date |
|---|---|---|
| feed: change /f/ to /n/. (need) | | |
| dart: change /ar/ to /ur/. (dirt) | | |
| saw: change /â/ to / /. (so) | | |
| cheer: change /ch/ to /sn/. (sneer) | | |
| pest: change /st/ to /n/. (pen) | | |
| brake: change /br/ to /sh/. (shake) | | |
| brook: change /oͦo / to / /. (broke) | | |
| both: change / / to /o͞o/. (booth) | | |
| then: change /e/ to /a/. (than) | | |
| bunch: change /b/ to /kr/. (crunch) | | |
| treat: change /tr/ to /wh/. (wheat) | | |
| spoil: change /oi/ to /o͞o/. (spool) | | |
| **Score** | /12 | /12 |

Observations: _____

_____

_____

_____

_____

_____

_____

# Letter Recognition Pretests and Posttests

Student _____

**Directions:** Ask the student to point to each letter, moving across the page, and name each one. If the student comes to a letter he or she doesn't know, say the letter name, put an **X** next to the letter in the column, and have the student continue. If the student says an incorrect letter name, record what he or she says in the column.

| | Pretest Date _____ | Posttest Date _____ | | Pretest Date _____ | Posttest Date _____ | | Pretest Date _____ | Posttest Date _____ | | Pretest Date _____ | Posttest Date _____ |
|---|---|---|---|---|---|---|---|---|---|---|---|
| e | | | t | | | H | | | S | | |
| h | | | f | | | L | | | B | | |
| m | | | l | | | U | | | K | | |
| c | | | g | | | N | | | J | | |
| o | | | z | | | T | | | X | | |
| a | | | j | | | A | | | P | | |
| y | | | p | | | D | | | M | | |
| b | | | k | | | V | | | G | | |
| x | | | q | | | Z | | | C | | |
| i | | | r | | | R | | | Y | | |
| d | | | v | | | F | | | Q | | |
| n | | | s | | | O | | | E | | |
| u | | | w | | | W | | | I | | |

# Letter Naming

Student _____ Grade _____

| | Pretest<br>Date _____ | Posttest<br>Date _____ | | Pretest<br>Date _____ | Posttest<br>Date _____ |
|---|---|---|---|---|---|
| m | | | c | | |
| t | | | n | | |
| a | | | b | | |
| s | | | j | | |
| i | | | k | | |
| r | | | y | | |
| d | | | e | | |
| f | | | w | | |
| o | | | p | | |
| g | | | v | | |
| l | | | q | | |
| h | | | x | | |
| u | | | z | | |
| **Score** | /13 | /13 | **Score** | /13 | /13 |

# Consonant Sounds

Student _____

**Directions:** Have students point to each letter and tell you the sound each consonant stands for. Some letters stand for more than one sound. Note whether students say both sounds. Circle any letters they miss on the recording sheet.

|  | Pretest Date | Posttest Date |
|---|---|---|
| m: /m/ | | |
| s: /s/ /z/ | | |
| c: /k/ /s/ | | |
| v: /v/ | | |
| l: /l/ | | |
| g: /g/ /j/ | | |
| n: /n/ | | |
| d: /d/ | | |
| t: /t/ | | |
| j: /j/ | | |
| w: /w/ | | |
| p: /p/ | | |
| r: /r/ | | |
| b: /b/ | | |
| q: /kw/ | | |
| h: /h/ | | |
| z: /z/ | | |
| f: /f/ | | |
| k: /k/ | | |
| x: /ks/ | | |
| n: /n/ | | |
| **Score** | /21 | /21 |

Observations: _____

_____

# Consonant Blends

Student _____

**Directions:** Ask students what sound the underlined letters make. Then have them read the word. Put a ✔ if they get the sound right and a + if they read the word correctly. **Example**: Trip. *The underlined letters make the* /tr/ *sound. The word is* trip.

| | Pretest Date | | Posttest Date | |
|---|---|---|---|---|
| | Sound | Word | Sound | Word |
| brat | | | | |
| crab | | | | |
| drip | | | | |
| from | | | | |
| grab | | | | |
| prod | | | | |
| trim | | | | |
| blot | | | | |
| clam | | | | |
| flap | | | | |
| glad | | | | |
| plan | | | | |
| slid | | | | |
| scab | | | | |
| skid | | | | |
| smell | | | | |
| snap | | | | |
| spill | | | | |
| scrub | | | | |
| swell | | | | |
| staff | | | | |
| squid | | | | |
| strap | | | | |
| sprig | | | | |
| split | | | | |
| thrill | | | | |
| drift | | | | |
| Score | | /27 | | /27 |

Observations: _____

_____

# Consonant Clusters

Student _____

**Directions:** Ask the student what sound the underlined letters make. Then have them read the word. Put a ✓ if they get the sound right and a + if they read the word correctly. **Example**: Trip. *The underlined letters make the /tr/ sound. The word is* **trip**.

|  | Pretest<br>Date | Posttest<br>Date |
|---|---|---|
| he<u>ld</u> |  |  |
| fe<u>lt</u> |  |  |
| ju<u>mp</u> |  |  |
| gra<u>nd</u> |  |  |
| dri<u>nk</u> |  |  |
| be<u>nt</u> |  |  |
| a<u>sk</u> |  |  |
| cri<u>sp</u> |  |  |
| ca<u>st</u> |  |  |
| Score | /9 | /9 |

# Consonant Digraphs

Student _____

**Directions:** Ask the student what sound the underlined letters make. Then have them read the word. Put a ✔ if they get the sound right and a + if they read the word correctly. **Example**: Trip. *The underlined letters make the /tr/ sound. The word is* **trip**.

.

| | Pretest<br>Date | Posttest<br>Date |
|---|---|---|
| <u>ch</u>at | | |
| su<u>ch</u> | | |
| <u>sh</u>ed | | |
| di<u>sh</u> | | |
| hu<u>ng</u> | | |
| ba<u>th</u> | | |
| <u>th</u>in | | |
| <u>th</u>at | | |
| <u>wh</u>en | | |
| **Score** | /9 | /9 |

Observations: _____

_____

# Short Vowels

Student _____

**Directions:** Have the student point to each word and tell you the sound each vowel stands for in the word. Record the student's responses in the column.

| | Pretest<br>Date | Posttest<br>Date |
|---|---|---|
| m<u>a</u>t | | |
| r<u>u</u>b | | |
| g<u>e</u>t | | |
| h<u>o</u>t | | |
| f<u>i</u>t | | |
| **Score** | /5 | /5 |

Observations: _____

_____

# Long Vowels

Student _____

**Directions:** Ask the student to tell you what sound the underlined letters make and then to read the word. Place a ✓ next to each sound identified correctly. Place a + next to each word read correctly. **Example**: T<u>a</u>pe. *The underlined letter makes the /ā/ sound. The word is* **tape**.

| | Pretest Date | | Posttest Date | |
|---|---|---|---|---|
| | Sound | Word | Sound | Word |
| <u>c</u>ake | | | | |
| h<u>o</u>le | | | | |
| <u>b</u>ike | | | | |
| f<u>ee</u>t | | | | |
| b<u>oa</u>t | | | | |
| b<u>e</u> | | | | |
| fl<u>ea</u> | | | | |
| c<u>o</u>ld | | | | |
| g<u>o</u> | | | | |
| t<u>ie</u> | | | | |
| r<u>o</u>ll | | | | |
| pr<u>y</u> | | | | |
| bl<u>ow</u> | | | | |
| tr<u>ai</u>n | | | | |
| spr<u>ay</u> | | | | |
| k<u>i</u>nd | | | | |
| **Score** | /16 | /16 | /16 | /16 |

Observations: _____

_____

*Foundational Skills Assessments*

# r-Controlled Vowels

Student _____

**Directions:** Ask the student to tell you what sound the underlined letters make and then to read the word. Place a ✓ next to each sound identified correctly. Place a + next to each word read correctly. **Example**: T<u>oy</u>. *The underlined letters make the /oi/ sound. The word is* **toy**.

| | Pretest Date | | Posttest Date | |
|---|---|---|---|---|
| | **Sound** | **Word** | **Sound** | **Word** |
| sh<u>are</u> | | | | |
| fl<u>air</u> | | | | |
| sw<u>ear</u> | | | | |
| l<u>ear</u>n | | | | |
| st<u>er</u>n | | | | |
| s<u>oar</u> | | | | |
| ch<u>ore</u> | | | | |
| fl<u>oor</u> | | | | |
| th<u>ir</u>d | | | | |
| bl<u>ur</u> | | | | |
| h<u>er</u>d | | | | |
| sp<u>ar</u>k | | | | |
| th<u>or</u>n | | | | |
| **Score** | /13 | /13 | /13 | /13 |

Observations: _____

_____

# Variant Vowels

Student _____

**Directions:** Ask the student to tell you what sound the underlined letters make and then to read the word. Place a ✓ next to each sound identified correctly. Place a + next to each word read correctly. **Example**: T<u>oy</u>. *The underlined letters make the /oi/ sound. The word is* **toy**.

| | Pretest Date | | Posttest Date | |
|---|---|---|---|---|
| | **Sound** | **Word** | **Sound** | **Word** |
| st<u>a</u>ll | | | | |
| st<u>a</u>lk | | | | |
| c<u>au</u>ght | | | | |
| dr<u>aw</u> | | | | |
| fl<u>o</u>ss | | | | |
| s<u>o</u>ng | | | | |
| bl<u>ew</u> | | | | |
| dr<u>oo</u>l | | | | |
| cl<u>ue</u> | | | | |
| pr<u>u</u>ne | | | | |
| wh<u>o</u> | | | | |
| st<u>oo</u>d | | | | |
| c<u>ou</u>ld | | | | |
| ch<u>ow</u> | | | | |
| cr<u>ou</u>ch | | | | |
| j<u>oi</u>nt | | | | |
| pl<u>oy</u> | | | | |
| **Score** | **/17** | **/17** | **/17** | **/17** |

Observations: _____

_____

# Blending Sounds

Student _____

**Directions:** Have the student say each sound in the word and then blend the sounds. **Example:** bin: /b/ /i/ /n/, bin.

| | Pretest Date | Posttest Date | | Pretest Date | Posttest Date |
|---|---|---|---|---|---|
| lug: /l/ /u/ /g/ | | | jab: /j/ /a/ /b/ | | |
| rack: /r/ /a/ /k/ | | | hut: /h/ /u/ /t/ | | |
| hot: /h/ /ô/ /t/ | | | zap: /z/ /a/ /p/ | | |
| rot: /r/ /ô/ /t/ | | | led: /l/ /e/ /d/ | | |
| fog: /f/ /ô/ /g/ | | | quit: /kw/ /i/ /t/ | | |
| sum: /s/ /u/ /m/ | | | sill: /s/ /i/ /l/ | | |
| cog: /k/ /ô/ /g/ | | | kin: /k/ /i/ /n/ | | |
| yam: /y/ /a/ /m/ | | | bun: /b/ /u/ /n/ | | |
| | | | **Score** | /16 | /16 |

Observations:_____
_____

# Silent Letters

Student _____

**Directions:** Ask the student to tell you what sound the underlined letters make and then to read the word. Place a ✔ next to each sound identified correctly.
**Example:** <u>kn</u>it. *The underlined letters make the /n/ sound. The word is **knit**.*

|  | Pretest<br>Date | Posttest<br>Date |
|---|---|---|
| <u>kn</u>ow | | |
| <u>gn</u>at | | |
| <u>wr</u>ite | | |
| <u>kn</u>eel | | |
| <u>gn</u>ash | | |
| <u>wr</u>en | | |
| lam<u>b</u> | | |
| si<u>gn</u> | | |
| <u>kn</u>ack | | |
| <u>wr</u>ath | | |
| cli<u>mb</u> | | |
| **Score** | /11 | /11 |

Observations: _____

_____

# High-Frequency Words (Kindergarten)

**Directions:** Have the student put a finger on the first word on the student sheet and then read across the line, saying the words as quickly as possible. Count as incorrect any word the student misses or hesitates on before reading.

| | Pretest Date | Posttest Date | | Pretest Date | Posttest Date |
|---|---|---|---|---|---|
| is | | | look | | |
| a | | | he | | |
| the | | | go | | |
| has | | | put | | |
| and | | | want | | |
| of | | | this | | |
| with | | | she | | |
| see | | | saw | | |
| for | | | play | | |
| no | | | like | | |
| little | | | can | | |
| have | | | big | | |
| are | | | jump | | |
| said | | | one | | |
| I | | | two | | |
| you | | | what | | |
| me | | | we | | |
| come | | | | | |
| here | | | | | |
| to | | | | | |
| my | | | | | |
| | | | Score | /38 | /38 |

Observations: _____

_____

# Review High-Frequency Words (K–1)

Student _____

**Directions:** The following words are high-frequency words. The list includes any words for which students have not yet learned the sounds. Some of these words will become decodable once students have learned the sounds. Have the student put a finger on the first word on the student sheet and read across the line, saying each word quickly. Count as incorrect any word the student misses or hesitates on before reading.

| | Pretest Date | Posttest Date | | Pretest Date | Posttest Date |
|---|---|---|---|---|---|
| is | | | go | | |
| the | | | put | | |
| has | | | want | | |
| and | | | this | | |
| of | | | she | | |
| with | | | saw | | |
| see | | | now | | |
| for | | | like | | |
| no | | | can | | |
| have | | | home | | |
| are | | | they | | |
| said | | | went | | |
| you | | | good | | |
| me | | | was | | |
| come | | | be | | |
| here | | | we | | |
| to | | | there | | |
| my | | | then | | |
| look | | | out | | |
| he | | | **Score** | /39 | /39 |

Observations: _____

_____

# High-Frequency Words (Grade 1, First Half)

Student _____

**Directions:** The following words are high-frequency words. The list includes any words for which students have not yet learned the sounds. Some of these words will become decodable once students have learned the sounds. Have the student put a finger on the first word on the student sheet and read across the line, saying each word quickly. Count as incorrect any word the student misses or hesitates on before reading.

| | Pretest Date | Posttest Date | | Pretest Date | Posttest Date | | Pretest Date | Posttest Date |
|---|---|---|---|---|---|---|---|---|
| the | | | do | | | over | | |
| see | | | which | | | under | | |
| go | | | went | | | try | | |
| she | | | was | | | give | | |
| and | | | there | | | far | | |
| play | | | then | | | too | | |
| little | | | out | | | | | |
| you | | | who | | | | | |
| with | | | good | | | | | |
| for | | | by | | | | | |
| no | | | them | | | | | |
| jump | | | were | | | | | |
| one | | | our | | | | | |
| have | | | could | | | | | |
| are | | | these | | | | | |
| said | | | once | | | | | |
| two | | | upon | | | | | |
| look | | | hurt | | | | | |
| my | | | that | | | | | |
| come | | | because | | | | | |
| here | | | from | | | | | |
| to | | | their | | | | | |
| of | | | when | | | | | |
| what | | | why | | | | | |
| put | | | many | | | | | |
| want | | | right | | | | | |
| this | | | start | | | | | |
| saw | | | find | | | | | |
| now | | | how | | | Score | /64 | /64 |

Observations: _____

_____

# High-Frequency Words (Grade1, Second Half)

Student _____

**Directions:** These are words students will encounter in the decodable books and for which they have not yet learned the sounds. Many of these words will become decodable once students have learned the sounds. Have the student put a finger on the first word on the student sheet and read across the line, saying each word quickly. Count as incorrect any word the student misses or hesitates on before reading.

| | Pretest Date | Posttest Date | | Pretest Date | Posttest Date | | Pretest Date | Posttest Date |
|---|---|---|---|---|---|---|---|---|
| afer | | | move | | | eight | | |
| call | | | change | | | any | | |
| large | | | away | | | | | |
| her | | | every | | | | | |
| house | | | near | | | | | |
| long | | | school | | | | | |
| off | | | earth | | | | | |
| small | | | done | | | | | |
| brown | | | before | | | | | |
| work | | | about | | | | | |
| year | | | even | | | | | |
| live | | | walk | | | | | |
| found | | | buy | | | | | |
| your | | | only | | | | | |
| know | | | through | | | | | |
| always | | | does | | | | | |
| all | | | another | | | | | |
| people | | | wash | | | | | |
| where | | | some | | | | | |
| draw | | | better | | | | | |
| again | | | carry | | | | | |
| round | | | learn | | | | | |
| they | | | very | | | | | |
| country | | | mother | | | | | |
| four | | | father | | | | | |
| great | | | never | | | | | |
| boy | | | below | | | | | |
| city | | | blue | | | | | |
| laugh | | | answer | | | | | |
| | | | | | Score | | /60 | /60 |

Observations: _____

_____

# High-Frequency Words (Grade 2, First Half)

Student _____

**Directions:** These are words students will encounter in the decodable books and for which they have not yet learned the sounds. Many of these words will become decodable once students have learned the sounds. Have the student put a finger on the first word on the student sheet and read across the line, saying each word quickly. Count as incorrect any word the student misses or hesitates on before reading.

| | Pretest Date | Posttest Date | | Pretest Date | Posttest Date | | Pretest Date | Posttest Date |
|---|---|---|---|---|---|---|---|---|
| here | | | eight | | | when | | |
| look | | | find | | | work | | |
| me | | | good | | | always | | |
| play | | | house | | | any | | |
| said | | | laugh | | | blue | | |
| see | | | mother | | | buy | | |
| she | | | move | | | city | | |
| try | | | never | | | draw | | |
| about | | | once | | | four | | |
| because | | | round | | | great | | |
| after | | | small | | | how | | |
| before | | | their | | | live | | |
| call | | | too | | | another | | |
| do | | | walk | | | boy | | |
| earth | | | where | | | could | | |
| father | | | year | | | every | | |
| give | | | all | | | far | | |
| her | | | away | | | from | | |
| know | | | better | | | hurt | | |
| large | | | by | | | over | | |
| many | | | change | | | out | | |
| near | | | done | | | these | | |
| off | | | even | | | then | | |
| people | | | found | | | there | | |
| right | | | learn | | | went | | |
| school | | | only | | | who | | |
| that | | | long | | | your | | |
| two | | | now | | | above | | |
| under | | | our | | | began | | |
| very | | | some | | | different | | |
| again | | | them | | | they | | |
| below | | | through | | | were | | |
| carry | | | upon | | | which | | |
| does | | | was | | | why | | |
| | | | | | | **Score** | /102 | /102 |

Observations: _____

# High-Frequency Words (Grade 2, Second Half)

Student _____

**Directions:** These are words students will encounter in the decodable books and for which they have not yet learned the sounds. Many of these words will become decodable once students have learned the sounds. Have the student put a finger on the first word on the student sheet and read across the line, saying each word quickly. Count as incorrect any word the student misses or hesitates on before reading.

| | Pretest Date | Posttest Date | | Pretest Date | Posttest Date | | Pretest Date | Posttest Date |
|---|---|---|---|---|---|---|---|---|
| point | | | begin | | | field | | |
| river | | | children | | | heard | | |
| second | | | important | | | knew | | |
| song | | | letter | | | listen | | |
| think | | | open | | | morning | | |
| three | | | own | | | several | | |
| until | | | sound | | | area | | |
| watch | | | talk | | | ever | | |
| white | | | almost | | | hours | | |
| young | | | animal | | | measure | | |
| add | | | around | | | notice | | |
| between | | | body | | | order | | |
| close | | | color | | | piece | | |
| example | | | eye | | | short | | |
| food | | | form | | | today | | |
| group | | | high | | | true | | |
| hear | | | light | | | cried | | |
| home | | | story | | | figure | | |
| left | | | across | | | horse | | |
| mountain | | | become | | | since | | |
| music | | | complete | | | easy | | |
| night | | | during | | | sure | | |
| old | | | happened | | | whole | | |
| picture | | | hundred | | | among | | |
| sentence | | | problem | | | finally | | |
| spell | | | toward | | | brought | | |
| thought | | | study | | | front | | |
| together | | | wind | | | gave | | |
| while | | | against | | | warm | | |
| world | | | certain | | | dark | | |
| air | | | door | | | clear | | |
| along | | | early | | | explain | | |
| | | | | | **Score** | | /96 | /96 |

Observations: _____

_____

# Phonics Quick Check Instructions

## Pre/Post Phonics Assessment Instructions

1. Make a copy of the student sheet. Laminate if desired.
2. Make a copy of the teacher record form for each student.
3. Administer the assessment one-on-one.
4. Count a response correct if the student successfully segments and blends the word by word parts or syllables or reads it as a complete unit. Document any errors.
5. Stop the testing if the student misses ONE item. Begin instruction for explicit systematic instruction.
6. For intervention purposes, you may administer the whole pretest and analyze the results to determine if the student has mastered the skills or needs further instruction, reinforcement, or practice.

## Quick Check Assessment Instructions

1. Make a copy of the student sheet. Laminate if desired.
2. Make a copy of the teacher record form for each student.
3. Administer the Quick Check one-on-one.
4. For segmenting and blending, use the example word provided with the directions to ensure the student understands what to do. Count a response correct if the student successfully segments and blends the word by word parts or syllables or reads it as a complete unit. Document any errors.
5. For high-frequency words, have the student read each word as quickly as possible, documenting hesitations or misses.
6. Analyze the results to determine if the student has mastered the skills or needs further instruction, reinforcement, or practice.

# Pre/Post Phonics Assessment

Student _____

**Directions:** Have the student point to each word on the corresponding student sheet, segment the word parts or syllables, and blend them together. Put a ✓ if the student successfully segments and blends the word or reads it as a complete unit. If the student misses the word, record the error.

| | Pretest Date | Posttest Date |
|---|---|---|
| **Closed-Syllable Patterns** | | |
| clam | | |
| kept | | |
| limp | | |
| sock | | |
| brush | | |
| cactus | | |
| hiccup | | |
| consent | | |
| **CVCe Syllable Patterns** | | |
| made | | |
| smile | | |
| quote | | |
| tune | | |
| mistake | | |
| inside | | |
| tadpole | | |
| excuse | | |
| **Open-Syllable Patterns** | | |
| be | | |
| so | | |
| pry | | |
| lady | | |
| silent | | |
| **Score** | /21 | /21 |

Observations: _____

_____

# Pre/Post Phonics Assessment

Student _____

**Directions**: Have the student point to each word on the corresponding student sheet, segment the word parts or syllables, and blend them together. Put a ✓ if the student successfully segments and blends the word or reads it as a complete unit. If the student misses the word, record the error.

| | Pretest<br>Date | Posttest<br>Date |
|---|---|---|
| **Long a Digraph Syllable Patterns** | | |
| mail | | |
| sway | | |
| they | | |
| weigh | | |
| detail | | |
| playmate | | |
| obey | | |
| eighty | | |
| **Long o Digraph Syllable Patterns** | | |
| throat | | |
| flown | | |
| foe | | |
| below | | |
| foamy | | |
| rowboat | | |
| **Long e Digraph Syllable Patterns** | | |
| treat | | |
| sneeze | | |
| grief | | |
| easy | | |
| between | | |
| relief | | |
| people | | |
| hockey | | |
| **Long i Digraph Syllable Patterns** | | |
| thigh | | |
| pie | | |
| brighten | | |
| design | | |
| untie | | |
| twilight | | |
| **Score** | /28 | /28 |

Observations: _____

_____

# Pre/Post Phonics Assessment

Student _____

**Directions**: Have the student point to each word on the corresponding student sheet, segment the word parts or syllables, and blend them together. Put a ✔ if the student successfully segments and blends the word or reads it as a complete unit. If the student misses the word, record the error.

| | Pretest Date | Posttest Date |
|---|---|---|
| **r-Controlled a Syllable Patterns** | | |
| charm | | |
| star | | |
| artist | | |
| racecar | | |
| **r-Controlled o Syllable Patterns** | | |
| storm | | |
| wore | | |
| pour | | |
| forest | | |
| explore | | |
| yourself | | |
| **r-Controlled e, i, u Syllable Patterns** | | |
| learn | | |
| serve | | |
| twirl | | |
| surf | | |
| early | | |
| perfect | | |
| thirsty | | |
| turnip | | |
| **r-Controlled /âr/ Syllable Patterns** | | |
| share | | |
| fair | | |
| wear | | |
| prepare | | |
| stairway | | |
| bearskin | | |
| **Score** | /24 | /24 |

Observations: _____

_____

# Pre/Post Phonics Assessment

Student _____

**Directions:** Have the student point to each word on the corresponding student sheet, segment the word parts or syllables, and blend them together. Put a ✓ if the student successfully segments and blends the word or reads it as a complete unit. If the student misses the word, record the error.

| | Pretest Date | Posttest Date |
|---|---|---|
| **Vowel Diphthong /oi/ Syllable Patterns** | | |
| moist | | |
| joy | | |
| poison | | |
| employ | | |
| **Vowel Diphthong /ou/ Syllable Patterns** | | |
| growl | | |
| pouch | | |
| towel | | |
| aloud | | |
| **Variant Vowel /o͞o/ Syllable Patterns** | | |
| crew | | |
| youth | | |
| glue | | |
| broom | | |
| chewy | | |
| regroup | | |
| pursue | | |
| cartoon | | |
| **Variant Vowel /o͝o/ Syllable Patterns** | | |
| shook | | |
| bush | | |
| pull | | |
| would | | |
| crooked | | |
| pushpin | | |
| bully | | |

| | Pretest Date | Posttest Date |
|---|---|---|
| **Variant Vowel /ô/ Syllable Patterns** | | |
| lawn | | |
| small | | |
| floss | | |
| walk | | |
| vault | | |
| sought | | |
| jigsaw | | |
| recall | | |
| bossy | | |
| salty | | |
| faultless | | |
| thoughtful | | |
| **Consonant +le Syllable Patterns** | | |
| wiggle | | |
| twinkle | | |
| fable | | |
| shuffle | | |
| **Score** | /39 | /39 |

Observations: _____

# Quick Check: Closed-Syllable Patterns

Student _____

Assessment Date _____

## Segmenting and Blending

**Directions:** Explain that these words use sounds the student has been learning. Have the student point to each word on the corresponding student sheet, segment the word parts or syllables, and blend them together. Put a ✓ if the student successfully segments and blends the word or reads it as a complete unit. If the student misses the word, record the error. **Example:** trot

| just | | helmet | |
|------|--|--------|--|
| miss | | problem | |
| batch | | ribbon | |
| tend | | pencil | |
| | | Score | /8 |

# Quick Check: CVCe Syllable Patterns

Student _____

Assessment Date _____

## Segmenting and Blending

**Directions:** Explain that these words use sounds the student has been learning. Have the student point to each word on the corresponding student sheet, segment the word parts or syllables, and blend them together. Put a ✓ if the student successfully segments and blends the word or reads it as a complete unit. If the student misses the word, record the error. **Example:** shone

| cute | | handshake | |
|------|--|-----------|--|
| stripe | | explode | |
| plane | | sunrise | |
| froze | | nickname | |
| | | Score | /8 |

# Quick Check: Open-Syllable Patterns

Student _____

Assessment Date _____

## Segmenting and Blending

**Directions:** Explain that these words use sounds the student has been learning. Have the student point to each word on the corresponding student sheet, segment the word parts or syllables, and blend them together. Put a ✓ if the student successfully segments and blends the word or reads it as a complete unit. If the student misses the word, record the error. **Example:** shy

| | | | |
|---|---|---|---|
| soda | | wavy | |
| zero | | silo | |
| pony | | ply | |
| spry | | whiny | |
| | | Score | /8 |

---

# Quick Check: Long a Digraph Syllable Patterns

Student _____

Assessment Date _____

## Segmenting and Blending

**Directions:** Explain that these words use sounds the student has been learning. Have the student point to each word on the corresponding student sheet, segment the word parts or syllables, and blend them together. Put a ✓ if the student successfully segments and blends the word or reads it as a complete unit. If the student misses the word, record the error. **Example:** bait

| | | | |
|---|---|---|---|
| maybe | | delay | |
| gray | | crayon | |
| mailman | | frail | |
| sleigh | | convey | |
| | | Score | /8 |

# Quick Check: Long o Digraph Syllable Patterns

Student _____

Assessment Date _____

## Segmenting and Blending

**Directions:** Explain that these words use sounds the student has been learning. Have the student point to each word on the corresponding student sheet, segment the word parts or syllables, and blend them together. Put a ✓ if the student successfully segments and blends the word or reads it as a complete unit. If the student misses the word, record the error. **Example:** loaf

| | | | |
|---|---|---|---|
| boast | | rainbow | |
| fishbowl | | poach | |
| known | | bestow | |
| floe | | coax | |
| | | Score | /8 |

---

# Quick Check: Long e Digraph Syllable Patterns

Student _____

Assessment Date _____

## Segmenting and Blending

**Directions:** Explain that these words use sounds the student has been learning. Have the student point to each word on the corresponding student sheet, segment the word parts or syllables, and blend them together. Put a ✓ if the student successfully segments and blends the word or reads it as a complete unit. If the student misses the word, record the error. **Example:** knead

| | | | |
|---|---|---|---|
| reveal | | chief | |
| pinwheel | | seacoast | |
| monkey | | upkeep | |
| screech | | belief | |
| | | Score | /8 |

# Quick Check: Long i Digraph Syllable Patterns

Student _____

Assessment Date _____

## Segmenting and Blending

**Directions:** Explain that these words use sounds the student has been learning. Have the student point to each word on the corresponding student sheet, segment the word parts or syllables, and blend them together. Put a ✔ if the student successfully segments and blends the word or reads it as a complete unit. If the student misses the word, record the error. **Example:** knight

| potpie | | highlight | |
|---|---|---|---|
| blight | | nigh | |
| frighten | | weeknight | |
| insight | | lie | |
| | | Score | /8 |

---

# Quick Check: r-Controlled a Syllable Patterns

Student _____

Assessment Date _____

## Segmenting and Blending

**Directions:** Explain that these words use sounds the student has been learning. Have the student point to each word on the corresponding student sheet, segment the word parts or syllables, and blend them together. Put a ✔ if the student successfully segments and blends the word or reads it as a complete unit. If the student misses the word, record the error. **Example:** chart

| embark | | arch | |
|---|---|---|---|
| alarm | | arctic | |
| yarn | | pardon | |
| boxcar | | radar | |
| | | Score | /8 |

# Quick Check: r-Controlled o Syllable Patterns

Student _____

Assessment Date _____

## Segmenting and Blending

**Directions:** Explain that these words use sounds the student has been learning. Have the student point to each word on the corresponding student sheet, segment the word parts or syllables, and blend them together. Put a ✓ if the student successfully segments and blends the word or reads it as a complete unit. If the student misses the word, record the error. **Example:** porch

| | | | |
|---|---|---|---|
| distort | | inform | |
| implore | | adorn | |
| pore | | carport | |
| format | | ashore | |
| | | **Score** | **/8** |

---

# Quick Check: r-Controlled e, i, u Syllable Patterns

Student _____

Assessment Date _____

## Segmenting and Blending

**Directions:** Explain that these words use sounds the student has been learning. Have the student point to each word on the corresponding student sheet, segment the word parts or syllables, and blend them together. Put a ✓ if the student successfully segments and blends the word or reads it as a complete unit. If the student misses the word, record the error. **Example:** yearn

| | | | |
|---|---|---|---|
| squirm | | bird | |
| occur | | disturb | |
| adverb | | prefer | |
| earn | | return | |
| | | **Score** | **/8** |

# Quick Check: r-Controlled /ar/ Syllable Patterns

Student _____

Assessment Date _____

## Segmenting and Blending

**Directions:** Explain that these words use sounds the student has been learning. Have the student point to each word on the corresponding student sheet, segment the word parts or syllables, and blend them together. Put a ✓ if the student successfully segments and blends the word or reads it as a complete unit. If the student misses the word, record the error. **Example:** lair

| | | | |
|---|---|---|---|
| rainwear | | impair | |
| compare | | swear | |
| spare | | party | |
| airfare | | aware | |
| | | **Score** | **/8** |

---

# Quick Check: Vowel Diphthong /oi/ Syllable Patterns

Student _____

Assessment Date _____

## Segmenting and Blending

**Directions:** Explain that these words use sounds the student has been learning. Have the student point to each word on the corresponding student sheet, segment the word parts or syllables, and blend them together. Put a ✓ if the student successfully segments and blends the word or reads it as a complete unit. If the student misses the word, record the error. **Example:** spoil

| | | | |
|---|---|---|---|
| annoy | | turquoise | |
| sirloin | | ploy | |
| loyal | | rejoice | |
| charbroil | | decoy | |
| | | **Score** | **/8** |

# Quick Check: Vowel Diphthong /ou/ Syllable Patterns

Student _____

Assessment Date _____

## Segmenting and Blending

**Directions:** Explain that these words use sounds the student has been learning. Have the student point to each word on the corresponding student sheet, segment the word parts or syllables, and blend them together. Put a ✓ if the student successfully segments and blends the word or reads it as a complete unit. If the student misses the word, record the error. **Example:** crouch

| | | | |
|---|---|---|---|
| aloud | | scowl | |
| chowder | | bouncy | |
| flounce | | turnout | |
| greyhound | | account | |
| | | Score | /8 |

---

# Quick Check: Variant Vowel /o͞o/ Syllable Patterns

Student _____

Assessment Date _____

## Segmenting and Blending

**Directions:** Explain that these words use sounds the student has been learning. Have the student point to each word on the corresponding student sheet, segment the word parts or syllables, and blend them together. Put a ✓ if the student successfully segments and blends the word or reads it as a complete unit. If the student misses the word, record the error. **Example:** crew

| | | | |
|---|---|---|---|
| roomy | | flue | |
| mildew | | foolish | |
| soundproof | | blue | |
| subdue | | moody | |
| | | Score | /8 |

# Quick Check: Variant Vowel /o͝o/ Syllable Patterns

Student _____

Assessment Date _____

## Segmenting and Blending

**Directions:** Explain that these words use sounds the student has been learning. Have the student point to each word on the corresponding student sheet, segment the word parts or syllables, and blend them together. Put a ✓ if the student successfully segments and blends the word or reads it as a complete unit. If the student misses the word, record the error. **Example:** wooly

| | | | |
|---|---|---|---|
| bull | | push | |
| childhood | | mistook | |
| bushy | | pulley | |
| checkbook | | output | |
| | | Score | /8 |

---

# Quick Check: Variant Vowel /ô/ Syllable Patterns

Student _____

Assessment Date _____

## Segmenting and Blending

**Directions:** Explain that these words use sounds the student has been learning. Have the student point to each word on the corresponding student sheet, segment the word parts or syllables, and blend them together. Put a ✓ if the student successfully segments and blends the word or reads it as a complete unit. If the student misses the word, record the error. **Example:** straw

| | | | |
|---|---|---|---|
| exhaust | | halter | |
| cobalt | | mall | |
| lawful | | withdraw | |
| gauze | | fault | |
| | | Score | /8 |

# Quick Check: Consonant +le Syllable Patterns

Student _____

Assessment Date _____

## Segmenting and Blending

**Directions:** Explain that these words use sounds the student has been learning. Have the student point to each word on the corresponding student sheet, segment the word parts or syllables, and blend them together. Put a ✓ if the student successfully segments and blends the word or reads it as a complete unit. If the student misses the word, record the error. **Example:** bauble

| | | | |
|---|---|---|---|
| treble | | straggle | |
| quibble | | speckle | |
| topple | | trifle | |
| shuffle | | bubble | |
| | | **Score** | **/8** |

# Word Study Quick Check Instructions

## Pre/Post Phonics Assessment Instructions

1. Make a copy of the student sheet. Laminate if desired.
2. Make a copy of the teacher record form for each student.
3. Administer the assessment one-on-one.
4. Count a response correct if the student successfully segments and blends the word by word parts or syllables or reads it as a complete unit. Document any errors.
5. Stop the testing if the student misses ONE item. Begin instruction for explicit systematic instruction.
6. For intervention purposes, you may administer the whole pretest and analyze the results to determine if the student has mastered the unit skills or needs further instruction, reinforcement, or practice.

## Quick Check Assessment Instructions

1. Make a copy of the student sheet. Laminate if desired.
2. Make a copy of the teacher record form for each student.
3. Administer the Quick Check one-on-one.
4. For segmenting and blending, use the example word provided with the directions to ensure the student understands what to do. Count a response as correct if the student successfully segments and blends the word by word parts or syllables or reads it as a complete unit. Document any errors.
5. For high-frequency words, have the student read each word as quickly as possible, documenting hesitations or misses.
6. Analyze the results to determine if the student has mastered the skills or needs further instruction, reinforcement, or practice.

# Noun Plurals: Pre/Post Phonics Assessment

Student _____

**Directions:** Have the student point to each word on the corresponding student sheet, segment the word parts or syllables, and blend them together. Put a ✓ if the student successfully segments and blends the word or reads it as a complete unit. If the student misses the word, record the error.

| | Pretest Date | Posttest Date |
|---|---|---|
| **Regular plurals** | | |
| stones | | |
| papers | | |
| lunches | | |
| ponies | | |
| **Irregular plurals** | | |
| mice | | |
| geese | | |
| knives | | |
| children | | |
| women | | |
| oxen | | |
| **Score** | /10 | /10 |

# Quick Check: Regular Plurals

Student _____

Assessment Date _____

## Segmenting and Blending

**Directions:** Explain that these words use sounds the student has been learning. Have the student point to each word on the corresponding student sheet, segment the word parts or syllables, and blend them together. Put a ✔ if the student successfully segments and blends the word or reads it as a complete unit. If the student misses the word, record the error. **Example:** scrapbooks

| | | | |
|---|---|---|---|
| wishes | | stories | |
| daisies | | monsters | |
| pencils | | bosses | |
| waltzes | | puppies | |
| | | Score | /8 |

---

# Quick Check: Irregular Plurals

Student _____

Assessment Date _____

## Segmenting and Blending

**Directions:** Explain that these words use sounds the student has been learning. Have the student point to each word on the corresponding student sheet, segment the word parts or syllables, and blend them together. Put a ✔ if the student successfully segments and blends the word or reads it as a complete unit. If the student misses the word, record the error. **Example:** radii

| | | | |
|---|---|---|---|
| cod | | men | |
| cacti | | lives | |
| salmon | | bass | |
| feet | | thieves | |
| | | Score | /8 |

# Words with Inflectional Endings: Pre/Post Phonics Assessment

Student _____

**Directions:** Have the student point to each word on the corresponding student sheet, segment the word parts or syllables, and blend them together. Put a ✓ if the student successfully segments and blends the word or reads it as a complete unit. If the student misses the word, record the error.

| | Pretest Date | Posttest Date |
|---|---|---|
| **-ed, -ing endings** | | |
| played | | |
| stacked | | |
| graded | | |
| trusting | | |
| planning | | |
| joking | | |
| Score | /6 | /6 |

---

# Quick Check: -ed, -ing endings

Student _____

Assessment Date _____

## Segmenting and Blending

**Directions:** Explain that these words use sounds the student has been learning. Have the student point to each word on the corresponding student sheet, segment the word parts or syllables, and blend them together. Put a ✓ if the student successfully segments and blends the word or reads it as a complete unit. If the student misses the word, record the error. **Example:** breaking

| | | | |
|---|---|---|---|
| trotted | | chopping | |
| diving | | crawled | |
| fished | | knitted | |
| smiled | | barked | |
| | | Score | /8 |

# Words with Prefixes: Pre/Post Phonics Assessment

Student _____

**Directions:** Have the student point to each word on the corresponding student sheet, segment the word parts or syllables, and blend them together. Put a ✓ if the student successfully segments and blends the word or reads it as a complete unit. If the student misses the word, record the error.

|  | Pretest Date | Posttest Date |
|---|---|---|
| **Prefix un-** | | |
| undo | | |
| untwist | | |
| unlucky | | |
| untangle | | |
| **Prefix re-** | | |
| repay | | |
| recall | | |
| relocate | | |
| reopen | | |
| **Prefix dis-** | | |
| dislike | | |
| dismiss | | |
| disconnect | | |
| disaster | | |
| Score | /12 | /12 |

# Quick Check: Prefix un-

Student _____

Assessment Date _____

## Segmenting and Blending

**Directions:** Explain that these words use sounds the student has been learning. Have the student point to each word on the corresponding student sheet, segment the word parts or syllables, and blend them together. Put a ✓ if the student successfully segments and blends the word or reads it as a complete unit. If the student misses the word, record the error. **Example:** unpack

| | | | |
|---|---|---|---|
| uncaught | | uncap | |
| unzip | | unedited | |
| unsalted | | unnamed | |
| unneeded | | unstack | |
| | | Score | /8 |

# Quick Check: Prefix re-

Student _____

Assessment Date: _____

## Segmenting and Blending

**Directions:** Explain that these words use sounds the student has been learning. Have the student point to each word on the corresponding student sheet, segment the word parts or syllables, and blend them together. Put a ✔ if the student successfully segments and blends the word or reads it as a complete unit. If the student misses the word, record the error. **Example:** rewind

| | | | |
|---|---|---|---|
| respect | | remove | |
| rejoin | | reclaim | |
| reshuffle | | refocus | |
| replace | | relax | |
| | | Score | /8 |

# Quick Check: Prefix dis-

Student _____

Assessment Date _____

## Segmenting and Blending

**Directions:** Explain that these words use sounds the student has been learning. Have the student point to each word on the corresponding student sheet, segment the word parts or syllables, and blend them together. Put a ✔ if the student successfully segments and blends the word or reads it as a complete unit. If the student misses the word, record the error. **Example:** dislike

| | | | |
|---|---|---|---|
| disagree | | disloyal | |
| disrupted | | disown | |
| disband | | distrusted | |
| disposed | | disappear | |
| | | Score | /8 |

# Words with Suffixes: Pre/Post Phonics Assessment

Student _____

**Directions:** Have the student point to each word on the corresponding student sheet, segment the word parts or syllables, and blend them together. Put a ✓ if the student successfully segments and blends the word or reads it as a complete unit. If the student misses the word, record the error.

| | Pretest<br>Date | Posttest<br>Date |
|---|---|---|
| **Suffix -less** | | |
| pointless | | |
| seedless | | |
| toothless | | |
| penniless | | |
| **Suffixes -sion, -tion, -ion** | | |
| question | | |
| division | | |
| companion | | |
| suggestion | | |
| confusion | | |
| suspicion | | |
| **Score** | /10 | /10 |

# Quick Check: Suffix -less

Student _____

Assessment Date _____

## Segmenting and Blending

**Directions:** Explain that these words use sounds the student has been learning. Have the student point to each word on the corresponding student sheet, segment the word parts or syllables, and blend them together. Put a ✓ if the student successfully segments and blends the word or reads it as a complete unit. If the student misses the word, record the error. **Example:** backless

| | | | |
|---|---|---|---|
| odorless | | spotless | |
| joyless | | boundless | |
| fearless | | flawless | |
| paperless | | thoughtless | |
| | | Score | /8 |

---

# Quick Check: Suffix -sion, -tion, -ion

Student _____

Assessment Date _____

## Segmenting and Blending

**Directions:** Explain that these words use sounds the student has been learning. Have the student point to each word on the corresponding student sheet, segment the word parts or syllables, and blend them together. Put a ✓ if the student successfully segments and blends the word or reads it as a complete unit. If the student misses the word, record the error. **Example:** motion

| | | | |
|---|---|---|---|
| vision | | donation | |
| edition | | erosion | |
| illusion | | solution | |
| suspicion | | invasion | |
| | | Score | /8 |

# Words with Greek Roots: Pre/Post Phonics Assessment

Student _____

**Directions:** Have the student point to each word on the corresponding student sheet, segment the word parts or syllables, and blend them together. Put a ✓ if the student successfully segments and blends the word or reads it as a complete unit. If the student misses the word, record the error.

|  | Pretest Date | Posttest Date |
|---|---|---|
| **Greek Roots** | | |
| biology | | |
| diagram | | |
| microscope | | |
| thermometer | | |
| photography | | |
| geometry | | |
| telephone | | |
| digraph | | |
| program | | |
| grammar | | |
| zoology | | |
| graphic | | |
| **Score** | /12 | /12 |

# Quick Check: Greek Roots

Student _____

Assessment Date _____

## Segmenting and Blending

**Directions:** Explain that these words use sounds the student has been learning. Have the student point to each word on the corresponding student sheet, segment the word parts or syllables, and blend them together. Put a ✓ if the student successfully segments and blends the word or reads it as a complete unit. If the student misses the word, record the error. **Example:** thermosphere

| stethoscope | | biopsy | |
|---|---|---|---|
| pathology | | holograph | |
| visible | | photon | |
| diagram | | altimeter | |
| | | **Score** | /8 |

# Letter Recognition

e h m c o a y b x

i d n u t f l g z

j p k q r v s w

H L U N T A D V Z

R F O W S B K J X

P M G C Y Q E I

## Letter Naming

m      t      a      s      i

r      d      f      o      g

l      h      u      c      n

b      j      k      y      e

w      p      v      q      x

z

## Consonant Sounds

m      s      c      v      l

g      n      d      t      j

w      p      r      b      q

h      z      f      k      x

n

## Consonant Blends

brat    crab    drip    from    grab

prod    trim    blot    clam    flap

glad    plan    slid    scab    skid

smell    snap    spill    scrub    swell

staff    squid    strap    sprig    split

thrill    drift

## Consonant Clusters

he**ld**    fe**lt**    ju**mp**    gra**nd**    dri**nk**

be**nt**    a**sk**    cri**sp**    ca**st**

---

## Consonant Digraphs

**ch**at    su**ch**    **sh**ed    di**sh**    hu**ng**

ba**th**    **th**in    **th**at    **wh**en

## Short Vowels

m<u>a</u>t        r<u>u</u>b        g<u>e</u>t        h<u>o</u>t        f<u>i</u>t

---

## Long Vowels

c<u>a</u>ke        h<u>o</u>le        b<u>i</u>ke        f<u>ee</u>t

b<u>oa</u>t        b<u>e</u>        fl<u>ea</u>        c<u>o</u>ld

g<u>o</u>        t<u>ie</u>        r<u>o</u>ll        pr<u>y</u>

bl<u>ow</u>        tr<u>ai</u>n        spr<u>ay</u>        k<u>i</u>nd

## r-Controlled Vowels

share      flair      swear      learn

stern      soar      chore      floor

third      blur      herd      spark

thorn

## Variant Vowels

stall      stalk      caught      draw

floss      song      blew      drool

clue      prune      who      stood

could      chow      crouch      joint

ploy

## Blending Sounds

| | | | |
|---|---|---|---|
| lug | rack | hot | bun |
| rot | fog | sum | cog |
| yam | jab | hut | zap |
| led | quit | sill | kin |
| bun | | | |

## Silent Letters

| | | | |
|---|---|---|---|
| <u>kn</u>ow | <u>g</u>nat | <u>w</u>rite | <u>kn</u>eel |
| <u>g</u>nash | <u>w</u>ren | la<u>mb</u> | sig<u>n</u> |
| <u>kn</u>ack | <u>w</u>rath | cli<u>mb</u> | |

# High-Frequency Words (Kindergarten)

| | | | |
|---|---|---|---|
| is | a | the | has |
| and | of | with | see |
| for | no | little | have |
| are | said | I | you |
| me | come | here | to |
| my | look | he | go |
| put | want | this | she |
| saw | play | like | do |
| big | jump | one | two |
| can | what | we | |

| | | | | |
|---|---|---|---|---|
| is | the | has | and | of |
| with | see | for | no | have |
| are | said | you | me | come |
| here | to | my | look | he |
| go | put | want | this | she |
| saw | now | like | do | home |
| they | went | good | was | be |
| we | there | then | out | |

# High-Frequency Words (Grade 1, First Half)

| | | | | |
|---|---|---|---|---|
| the | see | go | she | and |
| play | little | you | with | for |
| no | jump | one | have | are |
| said | two | look | my | come |
| here | to | of | what | put |
| want | this | saw | now | do |
| which | went | was | there | then |

| | | | | |
|---|---|---|---|---|
| out | who | good | by | them |
| were | our | could | these | once |
| upon | hurt | that | because | from |
| their | when | why | many | right |
| start | find | how | over | under |
| try | give | far | too | |

| | | | | |
|---|---|---|---|---|
| after | call | large | her | house |
| long | off | small | brown | work |
| year | live | found | your | know |
| always | all | people | where | draw |
| again | round | they | country | four |
| great | boy | city | laugh | move |

| change | away | every | near | school |
|--------|------|-------|------|--------|
| earth | done | before | about | even |
| walk | buy | only | through | does |
| another | wash | some | better | carry |
| learn | very | mother | father | never |
| below | blue | answer | eight | any |

# High-Frequency Words (Grade 2, First Half)

| | | | | |
|---|---|---|---|---|
| here | look | me | play | said |
| see | she | try | about | because |
| after | before | call | do | earth |
| father | give | her | know | large |
| many | near | off | people | right |
| school | that | two | under | very |
| again | below | carry | does | eight |
| find | good | house | laugh | mother |
| move | never | once | round | small |
| their | too | walk | where | year |

| | | | | |
|---|---|---|---|---|
| all | away | better | by | change |
| done | even | found | learn | only |
| long | now | our | some | them |
| through | upon | was | when | work |
| always | any | blue | buy | city |
| draw | four | great | how | live |
| another | boy | could | every | far |
| from | hurt | over | out | these |
| then | there | went | who | your |
| above | began | different | they | were |
| which | why | | | |

# High-Frequency Words (Grade 2, Second Half)

| | | | |
|---|---|---|---|
| point | river | second | song |
| think | three | until | watch |
| white | young | add | between |
| close | example | food | group |
| hear | home | left | mountain |
| music | night | old | picture |
| sentence | spell | thought | together |
| while | world | air | along |
| begin | children | important | letter |

| | | | |
|---|---|---|---|
| open | own | sound | talk |
| almost | animal | around | body |
| color | eye | form | high |
| light | story | across | become |
| complete | during | happened | hundred |
| problem | toward | study | wind |
| against | certain | door | early |
| field | heard | knew | listen |

| | | | |
|---|---|---|---|
| morning | several | area | ever |
| hours | measure | notice | order |
| piece | short | today | true |
| cried | figure | horse | since |
| easy | sure | whole | among |
| finally | brought | front | gave |
| warm | dark | clear | explain |

| | | | |
|---|---|---|---|
| clam | kept | limp | sock |
| brush | cactus | hiccup | consent |
| made | smile | quote | tune |
| mistake | inside | tadpole | excuse |
| be | so | pry | lady |
| silent | | | |

| | | | |
|---|---|---|---|
| mail | sway | they | weigh |
| detail | playmate | obey | eighty |
| throat | flown | foe | below |
| foamy | rowboat | | |
| treat | sneeze | grief | easy |
| between | relief | people | hockey |
| thigh | pie | brighten | design |
| untie | twilight | | |

| | | | |
|---|---|---|---|
| charm | star | artist | racecar |
| storm | wore | pour | forest |
| explore | yourself | | |
| learn | serve | twirl | surf |
| early | perfect | thirsty | turnip |
| share | fair | wear | |
| prepare | stairway | bearskin | |

| | | | |
|---|---|---|---|
| moist | joy | poison | employ |
| growl | pouch | towel | aloud |
| crew | youth | glue | broom |
| chewy | regroup | pursue | cartoon |
| shook | bush | pull | would |
| crooked | pushpin | bully | |
| lawn | small | floss | walk |
| vault | sought | jigsaw | recall |
| bossy | salty | faultless | thoughtful |
| wiggle | twinkle | fable | shuffle |

## Quick Check: Closed-Syllable Patterns

just          miss          batch          tend

helmet        problem       ribbon         pencil

## Quick Check: CVCe Syllable Patterns

cute          stripe        plane          froze

handshake     explode       sunrise        nickname

## Quick Check: Open-Syllable Patterns

soda          zero          pony          spry

wavy          silo          ply           whiny

## Quick Check: Long a Digraph Syllable Patterns

maybe         gray          mailman       sleigh

delay         crayon        frail         convey

## Quick Check: Long o Digraph Syllable Patterns

boast      fishbowl      known      floe

rainbow      poach      bestow      coax

## Quick Check: Long e Digraph Syllable Patterns

reveal      pinwheel      monkey      screech

chief      seacoast      upkeep      belief

## Quick Check: Long i Digraph Syllable Patterns

potpie      blight      frighten      insight

highlight      nigh      weeknight      lie

## Quick Check: r-Controlled a Syllable Patterns

embark      alarm      yarn      boxcar

arch      arctic      pardon      radar

## Quick Check: r-Controlled o Syllable Patterns

distort    implore    pore    format

inform    adorn    carport    ashore

## Quick Check: r-Controlled e, i, u Syllable Patterns

squirm    occur    adverb    earn

bird    disturb    prefer    return

## Quick Check: r-Controlled /ar/ Syllable Patterns

rainwear     compare     spare     airfare

impair     swear     party     aware

## Quick Check: Vowel Diphthong /oi/ Syllable Patterns

annoy     sirloin     loyal     charbroil

turquoise     ploy     rejoice     decoy

## Quick Check: Vowel Diphthong /ou/ Syllable Patterns

aloud          chowder          flounce          greyhound

scowl          bouncy          turnout          account

## Quick Check: Variant vowel /o͞o/ Syllable Patterns

roomy          mildew          soundproof          subdue

flue          foolish          blue          moody

Foundational Skills Assessments

## Quick Check: Variant Vowel /o͝o/ Syllable Patterns

bull    childhood    bushy    checkbook

push    mistook    pulley    output

## Quick Check: Variant Vowel /ô/ Syllable Patterns

exhaust    cobalt    lawful    gauze

halter    mall    withdraw    fault

## Quick Check: Consonant +le Syllable Patterns

treble          quibble          topple          shuffle

straggle          speckle          trifle          bubble

## Noun Plurals: Pre/Post Phonics Assessment

stones          papers          lunches          ponies

mice          geese          knives          children

women          oxen

## Quick Check: Regular Plurals

wishes     daisies     pencils     waltzes

stories     monsters     bosses     puppies

## Quick Check: Irregular Plurals

cod     cacti     salmon     feet

men     lives     bass     thieves

played     stacked     graded     trusting

planning   joking

---

## Quick Check: -ed, -ing endings

trotted        diving        fished        smiled

chopping    crawled       knitted     barked

# Words with Prefixes: Pre/Post Phonics Assessment

| | | | |
|---|---|---|---|
| undo | untwist | unlucky | untangle |

| | | | |
|---|---|---|---|
| repay | recall | relocate | reopen |

| | | | |
|---|---|---|---|
| dislike | dismiss | disconnect | disaster |

## Quick Check: Prefix un-

| | | | |
|---|---|---|---|
| uncaught | unzip | unsalted | unneeded |

| | | | |
|---|---|---|---|
| uncap | unedited | unnamed | unstack |

## Quick Check: Prefix re-

respect     rejoin     reshuffle  replace

remove     reclaim     refocus     relax

---

## Quick Check: Prefix dis-

disagree     disrupted     disband     disposed

disloyal     disown     distrusted     disappear

pointless    seedless    toothless    penniless

question    division    companion    suggestion

confusion    suspicion

## Quick Check: Suffix -less

odorless    joyless    fearless    paperless

spotless    boundless    flawless    thoughtless

---

## Quick Check: Suffix -sion, -tion, -ion

vision    edition    illusion    suspicion

donation    erosion    solution    invasion

biology   diagram   microscrope   thermometer

photography   geometry   telephone   digraph

program   grammar   zoology   graphic

## Quick Check: Greek Roots

stethoscope   pathology   visible   diagram

biopsy   holograph   photon   altimeter

# One-Minute Oral Reading Fluency Assessment

The One-Minute Oral Reading Fluency Quick Checks are used to evaluate students' reading rate, and to document their progress over time in comparison to national fluency norms. These quick checks can be used to gather information on students' oral fluency and phrasing. The quick checks determine the number of words the student reads correctly per minute and provide a rubric for assessing phrasing, pitch, stress, intonation, and comprehension. It is recommended that teachers formally assess students' reading fluency at the beginning, in the middle, and at the end of the school year. This information can become part of students' permanent portfolio for documentation and accountability. Students may be assessed individually when most convenient for teachers—at the beginning or end of the day, or when appropriate during a portion of small-group reading time, or when students are engaged in independent reading.

## Preparing to Administer One-Minute Oral Reading Fluency Quick Checks

Prior to administering the one-minute quick checks, copy the leveled passages and teacher recording forms for the target level(s). Then create a folder for each student. Throughout the year, store the students' quick checks in these folders, or place the quick checks in individual student portfolios.

## Instructions

Reading fluency, phrasing, and rate may be assessed whenever a student reads aloud. Use the procedure below to measure oral reading fluency.

1. Select the fluency quick check passage at the student's independent reading level (95–100% accuracy). You will also need a copy of the reproducible record form for that level.

2. Give the student a brief introduction to the passage. Ask the student to read the passage using his or her best voice.

3. As the student reads, mark any errors with a slash mark through the words. Errors are outlined in the scoring guidelines below.

4. At the end of one minute, mark the point in the text where the student was reading by circling the last word read. Allow the student to finish reading the passage.

5. Have students answer the self-check questions.

6. Count up the number of words read correctly. Record this information on the record form. Use the Reading Rate Goals chart on page 168 to compare the student's performance to the national norm for the grade level and time of year. Document this on the record form.

7. Use the Oral Fluency and Phrasing Rating Rubric on page 169 to rate the student's fluency and phrasing while reading.

## Scoring Guidelines

Words read correctly include words that are self-corrected within three seconds of an error. (Mark each self-correction with SC above the word.) Correctly read words that are repeated are not counted as errors.

Words read incorrectly should be marked with a /. The following errors are counted as incorrect:

- Mispronounced words—words that are misread.
- Word substitutions—one word read for another word. For example, **bold** for **ship**.
- Omissions or skipped words—words that are not read.
- Hesitations—If the student hesitates for three seconds or longer, say the word and have the student continue reading.

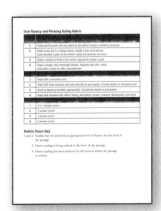

# Using Quick Check Results to Inform Instruction

Analyze quick check results to identify student strengths, needs, and next steps for instruction. Consider the following questions as you review and reflect on student performance.

*What does the oral reading fluency rubric show you about how a student is progressing as a reader? What areas are in need of additional support?*

*What connection between fluency and comprehension is evident?*

*How will results inform small-group instruction and individual reading conferences?*

## One-Minute Timed Reading Rate Goals

| Text Level | Grade Level | Reading Rate Goal (Words Per Minute) |
|---|---|---|
| D | First (beginning of year) | 20 |
| E | | 25 |
| F | | 30 |
| G | | 40 |
| H | | 50 |
| I | First (end of year) | 60 |
| J | Second (beginning of year) | 65 |
| K | | 75 |
| L | | 85 |
| M | Second (end of year) | 95 |
| N | Third (beginning of year) | 95 |
| O | | 105 |
| P | Third (end of year) | 115 |
| Q | Fourth (beginning of year) | 115 |
| R | Fourth (end of year) | 120 |
| S | Fifth (beginning of year) | 120 |
| T | | 125 |
| U | Fifth (end of year) | 130 |
| V | Sixth (beginning of year) | 135 |
| W | | 140 |
| X | Sixth (end of year) | 145 |
| Y | Seventh (beginning of year) | 145 |
| Z | Seventh (end of year) | 150 |

# Oral Fluency and Phrasing Rating Rubric

| Rating Scale | Phrasing and Fluency |
|---|---|
| 1 | Reads word by word. Does not attend to the author's syntax or sentence structures. |
| 2 | Reads slowly and in a choppy manner, usually in two-word phrases. Some attention is given to the author's syntax and sentence structures. |
| 3 | Reads in phrases of three or four words. Appropriate syntax is used. |
| 4 | Reads in longer, more meaningful phrases. Regularly uses pitch, stress, and author's syntax to reflect comprehension. |
| | **Intonation** |
| 1 | Reads with a monotone voice. |
| 2 | Reads with some intonation and some attention to punctuation. At times reads in a monotone voice. |
| 3 | Reads by adjusting intonation appropriately. Consistently attends to punctuation. |
| 4 | Reads with intonation that reflects feeling, anticipation, tension, character development, and mood. |
| | **Comprehension** |
| 1 | 0 or 1 answers correct |
| 2 | 2 answers correct |
| 3 | 3 answers correct |
| 4 | 4 answers correct |

## Rubric Score Key

1 and 2: Student has not achieved an appropriate level of fluency for the level of the passage.

3: Fluent reading is being refined at the level of the passage.

4: Fluent reading has been achieved for the level at which the passage is written.

# One-Minute Fluency Leveled Passages Quick Checks

Teacher Name_____ Grade Level _____

| Student Name | Beginning of Year Text Level/WPM | Mid-Year Text Level/WPM | End of Year Text Level/WPM |
|---|---|---|---|
| | | | |
| | | | |
| | | | |
| | | | |
| | | | |
| | | | |
| | | | |
| | | | |
| | | | |
| | | | |
| | | | |
| | | | |
| | | | |
| | | | |
| | | | |
| | | | |
| | | | |
| | | | |
| | | | |
| | | | |
| | | | |
| | | | |
| | | | |
| | | | |
| | | | |
| | | | |
| | | | |
| | | | |

Foundational Skills Assessments

# One-Minute Oral Reading Fluency Quick Check • Levels D–E (see p. 205)

Name:_____ Date:_____

Correct Words per Minute_____ National Norm of Words per Minute _____

## Playing Ball

| | |
|---|---|
| Tim and Jim play ball. They | _____6 |
| run. They jump. They throw | _____11 |
| the ball. They kick the ball. | _____17 |
| They have fun. | _____20 |
| | |
| "Time for bed!" says Mom. | _____25 |
| | |
| "Can we play more?" asks Tim. | _____31 |
| | |
| "You need to sleep now," | _____36 |
| says Mom. | _____38 |
| | |
| Tim and Jim go to bed. Mom | _____45 |
| tells them a story. The story | _____51 |
| is about two boys. The boys | _____57 |
| play ball. They run. They jump. | _____63 |
| They throw the ball. They kick | _____69 |
| the ball. The boys have fun. | _____75 |
| | |
| Tim and Jim smile. Soon the | _____81 |
| boys are asleep. | _____84 |

**Oral Reading Fluency Rubric**

| | Rubric Score | Comments: |
|---|---|---|
| **Phrasing and Fluency** | 1   2   3   4 | |
| **Intonation** | 1   2   3   4 | |
| **Comprehension** | 1   2   3   4 | |

**Rubric Score Key**
**1 and 2:** Student has not achieved an appropriate level of fluency for the level of the passage.
**3:** Fluent reading is being refined at the level of the passage.
**4:** Fluent reading has been achieved for the level at which the passage is written.

### Self-Check

1. Tim and Jim kicked the ball.
2. Mom said, "You need to sleep now."
3. Yes. Tim and Jim smiled.

Foundational Skills Assessments

Name _____ Date_____

Correct Words per Minute _____ National Norm of Words per Minute_____

## At the Park

| | |
|---|---:|
| You are at the park. | _____5 |
| What can you see? | _____9 |
| What can you hear? | _____13 |
| What can you touch? | _____17 |
| What can you smell? | _____21 |
| What can you taste? | _____25 |
| | |
| You see grass. You see trees. | _____31 |
| | |
| You hear kids. You hear dogs. | _____37 |
| | |
| You slide on the slide. | _____42 |
| You swing on the swings. | _____47 |
| | |
| You smell hot dogs. | _____51 |
| | |
| Get a hot dog. Taste | _____56 |
| the hot dog. Mmm! | _____60 |

**Oral Reading Fluency Rubric**

| | Rubric Score | Comments: |
|---|---|---|
| **Phrasing and Fluency** | 1  2  3  4 | |
| **Intonation** | 1  2  3  4 | |
| **Comprehension** | 1  2  3  4 | |

**Rubric Score Key**
**1 and 2:** Student has not achieved an appropriate level of fluency for the level of the passage.
**3:** Fluent reading is being refined at the level of the passage.
**4:** Fluent reading has been achieved for the level at which the passage is written.

Foundational Skills Assessments

Name _____ Date_____

Correct Words per Minute_____ National Norm of Words per Minute _____

## Water Fun

"Water, water, I love water!" _____5

said Lil. "I love to play in water." _____13

_____20

"I love to play in the sprinkler," _____22
said Tina.

"I love to play in the pool," _____29
said Kim. _____31

"I love to play in the lake," _____38
said Shane. _____40

"Water, water, I love water!" _____45

said Lil. "I love to play _____51

on water." _____53

"How can you play *on* water?" _____59

asked Shane. _____61

"Water can freeze," said Lil. _____66

"Then the water is ice. _____71

I can skate on ice!" _____76

**Oral Reading Fluency Rubric**

| | Rubric Score | Comments: |
|---|---|---|
| **Phrasing and Fluency** | 1  2  3  4 | |
| **Intonation** | 1  2  3  4 | |
| **Comprehension** | 1  2  3  4 | |

**Rubric Score Key**
**1 and 2:** Student has not achieved an appropriate level of fluency for the level of the passage.
**3:** Fluent reading is being refined at the level of the passage.
**4:** Fluent reading has been achieved for the level at which the passage is written.

Foundational Skills Assessments

# One-Minute Oral Reading Fluency Quick Check • Levels D–E (see p. 211)

Name_____  Date _____

Correct Words per Minute_____  National Norm of Words per Minute_____

## Here and There

| | |
|---|---|
| I like to go to school. | ____6 |
| I can walk to school. | ____11 |
| I can ride my bike to school. | ____18 |
| I like to go to my friend's house. | ____26 |
| My mom takes me in a car. | ____33 |
| A car can take you far away. | ____40 |
| Sometimes I ride a bus to | ____46 |
| my friend's house. A bus | ____51 |
| can take you far away. | ____56 |
| I like to go to my grandma's | ____63 |
| house. We take a train to | ____69 |
| her house. A train can take | ____75 |
| you far, far away. | ____79 |
| Sometimes we take a plane | ____84 |
| to my grandma's house. A | ____89 |
| plane can take you far, far | ____95 |
| away. | ____96 |

**Oral Reading Fluency Rubric**

| | Rubric Score | Comments: |
|---|---|---|
| **Phrasing and Fluency** | 1  2  3  4 | |
| **Intonation** | 1  2  3  4 | |
| **Comprehension** | 1  2  3  4 | |

**Rubric Score Key**
**1 and 2:** Student has not achieved an appropriate level of fluency for the level of the passage.
**3:** Fluent reading is being refined at the level of the passage.
**4:** Fluent reading has been achieved for the level at which the passage is written.

# One-Minute Oral Reading Fluency Quick Check • Levels F–G (see p. 213)

Name_____ Date _____

Correct Words per Minute _____ National Norm of Words per Minute_____

## The Moving Hat

| | |
|---|---:|
| Ann cannot find her cat. | _____5 |
| "Max!" Ann calls. "Where are | _____10 |
| you?" Max does not come. | _____15 |
| Ann looks for Max. Ann looks | _____21 |
| under her bed. Ann looks in | _____27 |
| the yard. She asks Mom and | _____33 |
| Dad, "Have you seen Max?" | _____38 |
| "No," say Mom and Dad. | _____43 |
| Ann goes to the living room. | _____49 |
| Her brother Mike is in the | _____55 |
| living room. Mike is looking at | _____61 |
| a hat. A hat is on the table. | _____69 |
| "What are you looking at?" | _____74 |
| Ann asks. | _____76 |
| "That hat keeps moving," | _____80 |
| says Mike. Ann looks at | _____85 |
| the hat. The hat *is* moving! | _____91 |
| Something is under the | _____95 |
| hat. Ann picks up the hat. | _____101 |
| "Max!" says Ann. "I have | _____106 |
| been looking for you." | _____110 |

**Oral Reading Fluency Rubric**

| | Rubric Score | Comments: |
|---|---|---|
| **Phrasing and Fluency** | 1  2  3  4 | |
| **Intonation** | 1  2  3  4 | |
| **Comprehension** | 1  2  3  4 | |

**Rubric Score Key**
**1 and 2:** Student has not achieved an appropriate level of fluency for the level of the passage.
**3:** Fluent reading is being refined at the level of the passage.
**4:** Fluent reading has been achieved for the level at which the passage is written.

### Self-Check

1. Ann could not find her cat.
2. The hat kept moving.
3. Ann called for Max. Ann looked all over.

Foundational Skills Assessments

Name _____ Date _____

Correct Words per Minute _____ National Norm of Words per Minute_____

## Juan Likes to Run

| | |
|---|---:|
| Juan likes to run. Juan runs | _____6 |
| by himself. He runs with his | _____12 |
| dog. He runs with his dad. | _____18 |
| He runs with his friends. | _____23 |
| | |
| When does Juan run? Juan | _____28 |
| runs in the morning. He runs | _____34 |
| in the afternoon. He runs in | _____40 |
| the evening. | _____42 |
| | |
| "I like to see you run, Juan," | _____49 |
| Mom says. | _____51 |
| | |
| "I *like* to run," Juan says, | _____57 |
| running around Mom. | _____60 |
| | |
| "Do you know what time | _____65 |
| it is?" Mom asks. | _____69 |
| | |
| Juan looks at the clock. He | _____75 |
| takes small, slow steps. His | _____80 |
| mother smiles. Juan stops | _____84 |
| running. It is time for bed! | _____90 |

**Oral Reading Fluency Rubric**

| | Rubric Score | Comments: |
|---|---|---|
| **Phrasing and Fluency** | 1   2   3   4 | |
| **Intonation** | 1   2   3   4 | |
| **Comprehension** | 1   2   3   4 | |

**Rubric Score Key**

**1 and 2:** Student has not achieved an appropriate level of fluency for the level of the passage.

**3:** Fluent reading is being refined at the level of the passage.

**4:** Fluent reading has been achieved for the level at which the passage is written.

### Self-Check

1. Juan likes to run.
2. Juan looked at the clock. It was time for bed.
3. Juan will run. He runs in the morning.

# One-Minute Oral Reading Fluency Quick Check • Level F (see p. 217)

Name_____ Date _____

Correct Words per Minute_____ National Norm of Words per Minute_____

## The Walking Bus

| | |
|---|---|
| Ten children at Park Lane School go | 7 |
| home in the walking bus. | 12 |
| Mrs. Green walks in front of | 18 |
| the bus. Mr. Scott walks in back of | 26 |
| the bus. The children walk in the | 33 |
| middle. | 34 |
| | |
| "Here we go!" says Mrs. Green. | 40 |
| "Look out for cars." | 44 |
| | |
| The bus walks slowly. It stops | 50 |
| at Ben's house. It stops | 55 |
| at Maria's house. It stops and stops | 61 |
| until all ten children | 66 |
| are home! | 68 |

**Oral Reading Fluency Rubric**

| | Rubric Score | Comments: |
|---|---|---|
| **Phrasing and Fluency** | 1  2  3  4 | |
| **Intonation** | 1  2  3  4 | |
| **Comprehension** | 1  2  3  4 | |

**Rubric Score Key**
**1 and 2:** Student has not achieved an appropriate level of fluency for the level of the passage.
**3:** Fluent reading is being refined at the level of the passage.
**4:** Fluent reading has been achieved for the level at which the passage is written.

## Self-Check

1. A walking bus takes children home from school.
2. Mrs. Green walked in front of the walking bus.
3. Ten children took the walking bus home.
4. The walking bus stopped at all the children's houses.

*Foundational Skills Assessments*

Name _____ Date _____

Correct Words per Minute_____ National Norm of Words per Minute_____

## The Biggest Sunflower

Children at Sunset School were — 5
growing sunflowers in the garden. — 10
They watered their sunflowers to — 15
help them grow. They talked to — 21
their sunflowers to help them — 26
grow. — 27

But Maria put her sunflower in — 33
a pot. All day long she moved the — 41
pot to follow the sunshine. — 46
Her sunflower grew very big. — 51
It became the biggest sunflower. — 56

"My sunflower likes sunshine," said — 61
Maria. "So where the Sun goes, my — 68
sunflower goes, too!" — 71

**Oral Reading Fluency Rubric**

| | Rubric Score | Comments: |
|---|---|---|
| **Phrasing and Fluency** | 1　2　3　4 | |
| **Intonation** | 1　2　3　4 | |
| **Comprehension** | 1　2　3　4 | |

**Rubric Score Key**
**1 and 2:** Student has not achieved an appropriate level of fluency for the level of the passage.
**3:** Fluent reading is being refined at the level of the passage.
**4:** Fluent reading has been achieved for the level at which the passage is written.

### Self-Check

1. The children grew sunflowers.
2. They watered their sunflowers and talked to them.
3. Maria put her sunflower in a pot.
4. She moved the pot to follow the sunshine.

# One-Minute Oral Reading Fluency Quick Check • Levels H–I (see p. 221)

Name_____ Date_____

Correct Words per Minute _____ National Norm of Words per Minute_____

## Whose Shadow

| | |
|---|---:|
| Kim, May, and Ben are playing. They | ____7 |
| are making shadows on the wall. They | ____14 |
| use their hands to make the shadows. | ____21 |
| "Look at my shadow!" says Kim. "Quack! | ____28 |
| My shadow is a duck." | ____33 |
| "Look at my shadow!" says May. "Meow! | ____40 |
| My shadow is a cat." | ____45 |
| "How about my shadow?" asks Ben. "Woof! | ____52 |
| My shadow is a little dog. Do you like | ____61 |
| my shadow?" | ____63 |
| "I like your shadow," says Kim. "But who | ____71 |
| is making the shadow of a *big* dog?" | ____79 |
| "Not me," says May. | ____83 |
| "Not me," says Ben. | ____87 |
| The children turn around. They see Ben's | ____94 |
| dog, Jake. Jake is making a shadow | ____101 |
| of his own. The children laugh. Jake is | ____109 |
| making the best shadow of all! | ____115 |

### Oral Reading Fluency Rubric

| | Rubric Score | Comments: |
|---|---|---|
| Phrasing and Fluency | 1  2  3  4 | |
| Intonation | 1  2  3  4 | |
| Comprehension | 1  2  3  4 | |

**Rubric Score Key**
**1 and 2:** Student has not achieved an appropriate level of fluency for the level of the passage.
**3:** Fluent reading is being refined at the level of the passage.
**4:** Fluent reading has been achieved for the level at which the passage is written.

### Self-Check

1. They were making shadows on the wall.
2. Kim's shadow was a duck. May's was a cat.
3. The kids did not know who was making the shadow of a big dog. They turned around and saw Jake making the shadow.

Name _____ Date_____

Correct Words per Minute_____ National Norm of Words per Minute_____

## Bird Rescue

Mom and I were in the yard. I saw a _____10
baby blue jay fly out of its nest. The _____19
baby bird landed on the grass. Then _____26
I saw Tabby, our cat! Tabby walked _____33
slowly toward the bird. _____37

"Mom! Tabby is going to get the baby _____45
bird!" I cried. _____48

Mom said, "Oh no! Save the bird!" _____55

Then we saw a big blue jay fly over _____64
Tabby's head. The big bird landed in _____71
the grass. Tabby ran toward the big _____78
bird. Tabby got very close. Then the _____85
big blue jay flew away. _____90

Tabby looked back at the baby bird. _____97
We looked, too. The baby bird flapped _____104
its tiny wings. Then the baby bird flew _____112
away! The big blue jay waited for the _____120
baby bird in the nest. _____125

The baby bird did not need our help _____133
after all. _____135

**Oral Reading Fluency Rubric**

| | Rubric Score | Comments: |
|---|---|---|
| **Phrasing and Fluency** | 1  2  3  4 | |
| **Intonation** | 1  2  3  4 | |
| **Comprehension** | 1  2  3  4 | |

**Rubric Score Key**
**1 and 2:** Student has not achieved an appropriate level of fluency for the level of the passage.
**3:** Fluent reading is being refined at the level of the passage.
**4:** Fluent reading has been achieved for the level at which the passage is written.

### Self-Check

1. A baby blue jay flew out of its nest.
2. The big blue jay flew away.
3. The big blue jay got Tabby away from the baby blue jay. The big blue jay showed the baby blue jay how to fly away.

Name _____ Date _____

Correct Words per Minute _____ National Norm of Words per Minute_____

## The Scruffy Dog

It was bath day for Mr. Green's dog.                         8
"Come here, Scruffy," said Mr. Green.                        14
"It's time for your bath."                                   19

Scruffy didn't like to be washed with dog                   27
soap. He didn't like to be brushed with                     35
a dog comb. He liked to be scruffy and                      44
dirty.                                                      45

"Here I come, Scruffy," said Mr. Green.                     52
"You can't run away from me this time."                     60

Scruffy ran into the yard and hid                           67
from Mr. Green. But Mr. Green found                         74
him, and now Scruffy is fluffy!                             80

**Oral Reading Fluency Rubric**

| | Rubric Score | Comments: |
|---|---|---|
| **Phrasing and Fluency** | 1  2  3  4 | |
| **Intonation** | 1  2  3  4 | |
| **Comprehension** | 1  2  3  4 | |

**Rubric Score Key**
**1 and 2:** Student has not achieved an appropriate level of fluency for the level of the passage.
**3:** Fluent reading is being refined at the level of the passage.
**4:** Fluent reading has been achieved for the level at which the passage is written.

### Self-Check

1. It was bath day.
2. Scruffy didn't like baths.
3. He hid in the yard.
4. He gave Scruffy a bath.

Name_____ Date_____

Correct Words per Minute_____ National Norm of Words per Minute _____

## The Sleepy Dog

| | |
|---|---|
| Sara had a cat, but she always wanted | 8 |
| to have a dog. "Jump, Snowy, jump," Sara | 16 |
| said to her cat. The cat just | 23 |
| went to sleep. "Sit, Snowy, sit," Sara said to | 32 |
| her cat. The cat just went to sleep. | 40 |
| | |
| Then Sara went with her mom to look after | 49 |
| her grandpa's dog. "Run after | 54 |
| the ball, Jack," Sara said to the dog. | 62 |
| | |
| He shut his eyes and went to sleep. | 70 |
| | |
| "Jack would make a very good cat!" said | 77 |
| Sara as she laughed. | 82 |

**Oral Reading Fluency Rubric**

| | Rubric Score | Comments: |
|---|---|---|
| Phrasing and Fluency | 1  2  3  4 | |
| Intonation | 1  2  3  4 | |
| Comprehension | 1  2  3  4 | |

**Rubric Score Key**
**1 and 2:** Student has not achieved an appropriate level of fluency for the level of the passage.
**3:** Fluent reading is being refined at the level of the passage.
**4:** Fluent reading has been achieved for the level at which the passage is written.

### Self-Check

1. Sara wanted a dog.
2. Sara and her mom went to take care of Sara's grandpa's dog.
3. Sara's cat always went to sleep.
4. Both the dog and the cat liked to go to sleep.

Name _____ Date_____

Correct Words per Minute_____ National Norm of Words per Minute_____

## The Painting

| | |
|---|---|
| Matt likes to paint. Matt paints pictures | _____7 |
| of things he sees outside. He paints | _____14 |
| pictures of cars. He paints pictures | _____20 |
| of trees. | _____22 |
| | |
| Meg is Matt's little sister. Meg watches | _____29 |
| Matt paint. "I want to paint, too," says | _____37 |
| Meg. "What can I paint?" | _____42 |
| | |
| Matt gets a big piece of paper. Matt | _____50 |
| puts the paper on the table. He gets | _____58 |
| some finger paints for Meg. He puts | _____65 |
| the finger paints on the table. | _____71 |
| | |
| "Now we can paint a picture together," | _____78 |
| says Matt. | _____80 |
| | |
| First Meg paints. Meg uses her hands. | _____87 |
| She makes green lines on the paper. | _____94 |
| "I see grass outside," says Meg. | _____100 |
| | |
| Then Matt paints. Matt uses a brush. | _____107 |
| He paints a flower in the grass! | _____114 |

**Oral Reading Fluency Rubric**

| | Rubric Score | Comments: |
|---|---|---|
| **Phrasing and Fluency** | 1  2  3  4 | |
| **Intonation** | 1  2  3  4 | |
| **Comprehension** | 1  2  3  4 | |

**Rubric Score Key**
**1 and 2:** Student has not achieved an appropriate level of fluency for the level of the passage.
**3:** Fluent reading is being refined at the level of the passage.
**4:** Fluent reading has been achieved for the level at which the passage is written.

### Self-Check

1. Matt paints pictures of things he sees outside.
2. Meg wanted to paint because she watched Matt paint.
3. Matt got paper and finger paints for Meg. He let Meg paint first. He painted a flower for Meg.

# One-Minute Oral Reading Fluency Quick Check • Levels J–K (see p. 231)

Name_____ Date _____

Correct Words per Minute_____ National Norm of Words per Minute _____

## Kim's Bad Day

| | |
|---|---|
| Kim had a bad day. First, her brother | ____8 |
| ate the last bowl of Silly Shapes cereal. | ____16 |
| Kim had to eat her mother's boring | ____23 |
| wheat flakes. Then Kim missed the bus. | ____30 |
| She had to get a ride from her dad. | ____39 |
| | |
| Ms. Lopez gave the class a spelling test. | ____47 |
| Kim looked at the test and frowned. | ____54 |
| She had studied the wrong list of | ____61 |
| words! Ms. Lopez drew a sad face | ____68 |
| on Kim's test. Kim wanted to cry. | ____75 |
| | |
| Kim went home and showed her mother | ____82 |
| the spelling test. Mom made a sad face | ____90 |
| like the one Ms. Lopez drew on the test. | ____99 |
| | |
| Kim walked slowly to her room. Her eyes | ____107 |
| filled with tears. Then she bumped into | ____114 |
| something big and furry. She bumped | ____120 |
| into her dog, Buddy. Kim showed Buddy | ____127 |
| the test. Buddy did not frown. Buddy | ____134 |
| tried to eat the test! Kim laughed and | ____142 |
| hugged her dog, her Buddy. | ____147 |

**Oral Reading Fluency Rubric**

| | Rubric Score | Comments: |
|---|---|---|
| **Phrasing and Fluency** | 1  2  3  4 | |
| **Intonation** | 1  2  3  4 | |
| **Comprehension** | 1  2  3  4 | |

**Rubric Score Key**
**1 and 2:** Student has not achieved an appropriate level of fluency for the level of the passage.
**3:** Fluent reading is being refined at the level of the passage.
**4:** Fluent reading has been achieved for the level at which the passage is written.

## Self-Check

1. Kim missed the bus.
2. Kim had studied the wrong list of words.
3. Buddy does not frown at Kim. Buddy makes Kim laugh. Buddy is her buddy.

Name _____ Date_____

Correct Words per Minute _____ National Norm of Words per Minute _____

## The Happy Robot

Robot sat down at the kitchen table. — 7

"Would you like something to eat?" asked — 14
Robot's owner. — 16

"No, I'm not hungry," said Robot. But then it — 25
ate 10 banana-nut muffins. "I — 29
want to look at some of your wires," — 37
said Robot's owner. She gently opened — 43
the door to Robot's tummy and looked — 50
inside. — 51

"Your wires are messed up, so you eat — 59
when you're not hungry." — 63

When Robot was fixed, it smiled and said, — 71
"Thank you for fixing me. Now I will not feel — 81
so stuffed." — 83

**Oral Reading Fluency Rubric**

| | Rubric Score | Comments: |
|---|---|---|
| **Phrasing and Fluency** | 1   2   3   4 | |
| **Intonation** | 1   2   3   4 | |
| **Comprehension** | 1   2   3   4 | |

**Rubric Score Key**
**1 and 2:** Student has not achieved an appropriate level of fluency for the level of the passage.
**3:** Fluent reading is being refined at the level of the passage.
**4:** Fluent reading has been achieved for the level at which the passage is written.

### Self-Check

1. Robot ate 10 banana-nut muffins.
2. It ate because its wires were messed up.
3. Robot's owner fixed it.
4. He wouldn't feel stuffed anymore.

Name _____ Date _____

Correct Words per Minute _____ National Norm of Words per Minute _____

## The Weather Watcher

The weather watcher watched the weather — 6
every day. He told people watching TV — 13
when it was going to be sunny, windy, — 21
rainy, or snowy. — 24

One day the weather watcher got tired — 31
of watching the weather. He decided he — 38
wanted to watch other things. So he went — 45
on vacation. — 48

He watched strong winds blow sailboats — 54
over in the sea. He watched heavy rain — 62
flood streets and sidewalks. Wherever he — 68
went, the weather caused problems. So — 74
he returned to watch the weather in — 81
order to warn people when bad weather — 88
was coming. — 90

**Oral Reading Fluency Rubric**

| | Rubric Score | Comments: |
|---|---|---|
| Phrasing and Fluency | 1  2  3  4 | |
| Intonation | 1  2  3  4 | |
| Comprehension | 1  2  3  4 | |

**Rubric Score Key**
**1 and 2:** Student has not achieved an appropriate level of fluency
for the level of the passage.
**3:** Fluent reading is being refined at the level
of the passage.
**4:** Fluent reading has been achieved for the level at which
the passage is written.

### Self-Check

1. He watched and reported the weather.
2. He got tired of doing it.
3. He saw strong winds blowing over sailboats and rain flooding streets.
4. He wanted to warn people when bad weather was coming.

# One-Minute Oral Reading Fluency Assessment Record • Levels L–M (see p. 237)

Name _____ Date _____

Correct Words per Minute_____ National Norm of Words per Minute _____

## All About Me

| | |
|---|---:|
| Lee's father was sitting in his favorite rocking | _____8 |
| chair. He was reading and smiling. "What are | _____16 |
| you reading?" Lee asked. | _____20 |
| | |
| "I'm reading a special book. The book is about | _____29 |
| a special person," said Lee's father. | _____35 |
| | |
| "Who is it?" Lee asked. Lee went up to the | _____45 |
| rocking chair and climbed onto her father's lap. | _____53 |
| | |
| Lee looked at the book. "The book has pictures | _____62 |
| of a baby," she said. "That baby is cute!" | _____71 |
| | |
| Lee's father said, "That baby is smart, too. That | _____80 |
| baby could say lots of words before age two. | _____89 |
| That baby even learned to walk all by herself." | _____98 |
| | |
| "Who is that cute, smart baby?" Lee asked. | _____106 |
| | |
| "It's you!" Lee's father said with a laugh. He | _____115 |
| hugged Lee. Lee hugged him back. | _____121 |

**Oral Reading Fluency Rubric**

| | Rubric Score | Comments: |
|---|---|---|
| **Phrasing and Fluency** | 1  2  3  4 | |
| **Intonation** | 1  2  3  4 | |
| **Comprehension** | 1  2  3  4 | |

**Rubric Score Key**
**1 and 2:** Student has not achieved an appropriate level of fluency for the level of the passage.
**3:** Fluent reading is being refined at the level of the passage.
**4:** Fluent reading has been achieved for the level at which the passage is written.

## Self-Check

1. Lee's father was reading a special book.
2. Lee sat on her father's lap and looked at the book.
3. Lee's father thought the baby was very special. The baby could say lots of words before age two. She learned to walk all by herself.

Name _____ Date _____

Correct Words per Minute_____ National Norm of Words per Minute _____

## Princess Brat

| | |
|---|---|
| Kate lived in a tiny house in the village. Kate | _____10 |
| was visiting Princess Brat's huge house for the | _____18 |
| first time. Kate brought a doll with her. "I want | _____28 |
| that doll," Princess Brat said. "Give her to me!" | _____37 |
| | |
| "No," Kate said calmly. "I will not give you my | _____47 |
| doll. But I will let you play with her." | _____56 |
| | |
| "You will let me play with your doll?" Princess | _____65 |
| Brat asked. | _____67 |
| | |
| "Sure," Kate said happily. | _____71 |
| | |
| Princess Brat was quiet. Then she said, "I will | _____80 |
| let you play with one of my dolls. Look inside | _____90 |
| my doll castle." | _____93 |
| | |
| "Wow! You have so many dolls!" Kate said. | _____101 |
| "I have only one doll." | _____106 |
| | |
| "Oh," said Princess Brat. She was quiet again. | _____114 |
| Then she said, "You can take some of my dolls | _____124 |
| home with you." | _____127 |
| | |
| Kate smiled and said, "You do not need a | _____136 |
| new doll, Princess Brat. But you *do* need | _____144 |
| a new name!" | _____147 |

**Oral Reading Fluency Rubric**

| | Rubric Score | Comments: |
|---|---|---|
| **Phrasing and Fluency** | 1  2  3  4 | |
| **Intonation** | 1  2  3  4 | |
| **Comprehension** | 1  2  3  4 | |

**Rubric Score Key**
**1 and 2:** Student has not achieved an appropriate level of fluency for the level of the passage.
**3:** Fluent reading is being refined at the level of the passage.
**4:** Fluent reading has been achieved for the level at which the passage is written.

## Self-Check

1. Princess Brat lived in a huge house.
2. Princess Brat lives in a huge house. Kate lives in a tiny house. Princess Brat has many dolls. Kate has one doll.
3. The princess told Kate she could take some of the dolls home. The princess was not acting like a brat.

Name_____ Date_____

Correct Words per Minute _____ National Norm of Words per Minute_____

## The Red Pig

The baby pink pig looked at the other pigs. — 9

"You all need a bath," she said. "I'm not — 18
smelly, and I don't have mud all over me. — 27
I'm lovely, clean, and pink." — 32

The other pigs looked at the baby pig. Then — 41
they looked up at the hot sun and smiled. — 50
Soon the baby pig got hotter and hotter. She — 59
also got pinker and pinker. The pigs said, — 67
"You're lovely and clean, but you're not pink. — 75
Your skin is red." — 79

So the baby red pig jumped into the brown — 88
mud and was never, ever pink or red again! — 97

**Oral Reading Fluency Rubric**

|  | Rubric Score | Comments: |
|---|---|---|
| Phrasing and Fluency | 1  2  3  4 |  |
| Intonation | 1  2  3  4 |  |
| Comprehension | 1  2  3  4 |  |

**Rubric Score Key**

**1 and 2:** Student has not achieved an appropriate level of fluency for the level of the passage.

**3:** Fluent reading is being refined at the level of the passage.

**4:** Fluent reading has been achieved for the level at which the passage is written.

## Self-Check

1. The baby pig is the main character.
2. The setting is the barnyard.
3. The other pigs were all muddy and smelly.
4. She jumped into the mud.

Name_____ Date _____

Correct Words per Minute _____ National Norm of Words per Minute_____

## Molly's Smile

Molly is 3 years old, and she doesn't talk very     9
much. When she was 2, her family waited and     17
waited for her to talk. But Molly just smiled and     27
didn't say much.     30

Molly's family took her to a children's doctor.     38
The doctor thought Molly just learned things     45
more slowly than other children. Molly didn't     52
talk to the doctor, but she gave him a big     62
smile.     63

Her family took her to a speech teacher, who     72
helped Molly learn how to say words. Slowly,     80
Molly started to catch up with other children.     88

Molly still likes smiling. Her smile speaks     95
1,000 words!     96

**Oral Reading Fluency Rubric**

| | Rubric Score | Comments: |
|---|---|---|
| Phrasing and Fluency | 1   2   3   4 | |
| Intonation | | |
| Comprehension | | |

**Rubric Score Key**

**1 and 2:** Student has not achieved an appropriate level of fluency for the level of the passage.

**3:** Fluent reading is being refined at the level of the passage.

**4:** Fluent reading has been achieved for the level at which the passage is written.

### Self-Check

1. The main character is Molly.
2. Molly was 3 years old and did not talk very much.
3. Molly's parents took her to a speech teacher.
4. Molly's smile speaks 1,000 words.

Name _____ Date _____

Correct Words per Minute_____ National Norm of Words per Minute _____

## Mom's Birthday

| | |
|---|---|
| Today was Mom's birthday, so Tammy and I got up | 10 |
| early to bake a cake. Tammy read the recipe. I got | 21 |
| out the flour, sugar, cocoa, and cooking oil. | 29 |
| | |
| "We also need two eggs, Sammy," said Tammy. I put | 39 |
| the eggs on the counter, but one egg rolled off. | 49 |
| | |
| "Oops!" I picked up the broken egg shell. "I'll clean | 59 |
| the rest later," I said. Then we poured everything into | 69 |
| a big metal bowl. We set the electric mixer on high. | 80 |
| | |
| "Oops!" I said again. Some of the cake batter flew | 90 |
| out of the bowl. "I think we should put the mixer on | 102 |
| *low*. We'll clean the walls later," I added. | 110 |
| | |
| We poured the rest of the batter into the pan and | 121 |
| put the pan in the oven. We baked the cake before | 132 |
| Mom woke up. She came into the kitchen just as we | 143 |
| were frosting the cake. | 147 |
| | |
| Boy, did Mom look surprised—and happy! | 154 |

**Oral Reading Fluency Rubric**

| | Rubric Score | Comments: |
|---|---|---|
| **Phrasing and Fluency** | 1   2   3   4 | |
| **Intonation** | 1   2   3   4 | |
| **Comprehension** | 1   2   3   4 | |

**Rubric Score Key**
**1 and 2:** Student has not achieved an appropriate level of fluency for the level of the passage.
**3:** Fluent reading is being refined at the level of the passage.
**4:** Fluent reading has been achieved for the level at which the passage is written.

## Self-Check

1. Sammy got out flour, sugar, cocoa, and cooking oil.
2. The kids set the electric mixer on high.
3. The kids baked a cake for her. They also made a mess!

Name_____ Date_____

Correct Words per Minute_____ National Norm of Words per Minute _____

## The Meeting of the Mount Rushmore Presidents

| | |
|---|---|
| Good morning, Tom. Good morning, Teddy. Good | ____7 |
| morning, Abe," said George | ____11 |
| "Good morning to you, too," said Tom, Teddy, | ____19 |
| and Abe. | ____21 |
| It was a beautiful morning at Mount Rushmore. | ____29 |
| Years ago, artists carved the faces of four presidents | ____38 |
| into the mountain. The sun lit up the faces of | ____48 |
| George Washington, Thomas Jefferson, Theodore | ____53 |
| Roosevelt, and Abraham Lincoln. | ____57 |
| George said, "We need to vote on adding another | ____66 |
| president's face to our monument." | ____71 |
| "Four presidents are enough," said Tom. "George | ____78 |
| and I helped start the country. Abe kept it together | ____88 |
| during the Civil War. And Teddy did a fine job | ____98 |
| helping the country grow." | ____102 |
| "We've discussed this already," said Abe. "We are | ____110 |
| presidents from the first 125 years of American | ____117 |
| history. We need to add a president from the past | ____127 |
| 100 years." | ____128 |
| Teddy agreed. "I was the twenty-sixth president. | ____135 |
| More than a dozen new presidents have come and | ____144 |
| gone since then," he said. | ____149 |
| "Surely one of them should have his face added | ____159 |
| to our monument," said George. "Whom would | ____166 |
| you suggest?" | ____168 |

**Oral Reading Fluency Rubric**

| | Rubric Score | Comments: |
|---|---|---|
| **Phrasing and Fluency** | 1  2  3  4 | |
| **Intonation** | 1  2  3  4 | |
| **Comprehension** | 1  2  3  4 | |

**Rubric Score Key**
**1 and 2:** Student has not achieved an appropriate
level of fluency for the level of the passage.
**3:** Fluent reading is being refined at the level
of the passage.
**4:** Fluent reading has been achieved for the
level at which the passage is written.

## Self-Check

1. It was a beautiful morning at Mount Rushmore.
2. Tom isn't sure about adding another president to Mount Rushmore, but the other presidents want to.
3. Answers will vary.

Name_____ Date _____

Correct Words per Minute _____ National Norm of Words per Minute_____

# The Rainbow Mailbox

Lana and her mom wanted to make a colorful — 9
mailbox. — 10

"What kind of mailbox do you want to build?" — 19
asked Lana's mom. "How about a dinosaur mailbox?" — 27

"That's not very colorful," replied Lana. "Why — 34
don't we build a rainbow mailbox of red, orange, — 43
yellow, green, blue, indigo, and violet?" — 49

"Then I think we'd better go to the paint store," — 59
said Lana's mom, laughing. — 63

"Oops, we need eight colors. I forgot about gold — 72
paint for the pot of gold that's at the end of the — 84
rainbow!" said Lana. — 87

When the mail carrier saw the rainbow mailbox, — 95
she said to Lana, "Your mailbox makes me cheerful — 104
on rainy days!" — 107

**Oral Reading Fluency Rubric**

|                        | Rubric Score | Comments: |
|------------------------|--------------|-----------|
| Phrasing and Fluency   | 1    2    3    4 |           |
| Intonation             | 1    2    3    4 |           |
| Comprehension          | 1    2    3    4 |           |

**Rubric Score Key**

**1 and 2:** Student has not achieved an appropriate level of fluency for the level of the passage.

**3:** Fluent reading is being refined at the level of the passage.

**4:** Fluent reading has been achieved for the level at which the passage is written.

## Self-Check

1. She thought it was not colorful enough.
2. They almost forgot the gold paint.
3. They needed the gold paint to paint a pot of gold at the end of the rainbow.
4. It made her feel cheerful on rainy days.

Name _____ Date _____

Correct Words per Minute _____ National Norm of Words per Minute_____

## Scarecrow Joe

The old crows weren't afraid of Scarecrow Joe.     8
Farmer Robin knew that she had to do something,     17
so she dressed Joe in black clothes.     24

"That will make you look scary," she said to     33
Scarecrow Joe.     35

But the crows thought that Joe looked like a big,     45
black, friendly bird. They just kept eating Farmer     53
Robin's corn.     55

One day an eagle flew over the field and saw the     66
crows eating Farmer Robin's corn. The eagle decided     74
to help poor, frightened Scarecrow Joe by swooping     82
down and scaring the crows.     87

The eagle said, "I'm an eagle who scares crows,"     96
and sat on Joe's shoulder. From that day on,     105
the eagle and the scarecrow kept Farmer Robin's     113
corn safe.     115

**Oral Reading Fluency Rubric**

| | Rubric Score | Comments: |
|---|---|---|
| Phrasing and Fluency | 1   2   3   4 | |
| Intonation | 1   2   3   4 | |
| Comprehension | 1   2   3   4 | |

**Rubric Score Key**

**1 and 2:** Student has not achieved an appropriate level of fluency for the level of the passage.

**3:** Fluent reading is being refined at the level of the passage.

**4:** Fluent reading has been achieved for the level at which the passage is written.

## Self-Check

1. The setting of the story is Farmer Robin's field.
2. Farmer Robin dressed him in black clothes.
3. The crows thought Scarecrow Joe looked like a big, friendly bird.
4. An eagle swooped down and scared away the crows.

# One-Minute Oral Reading Fluency Quick Check • Level P (see p. 253)

Name _____ Date_____

Correct Words per Minute _____ National Norm of Words per Minute_____

## The Cat Show

"I am going to enter Ebony in the big cat show, ⬤ 11
but first I have to give her a bath," said Jessie. ⬤ 22

Ebony sensed that she was about to get a bath and ⬤ 33
scrambled up a tall cottonwood tree. Jessie pleaded ⬤ 41
and pleaded for her to come down. But Ebony just ⬤ 52
sat high up in the tree, ignoring Jessie's pleas. All the ⬤ 62
neighbors came out and tried to help ⬤ 69
Jessie get Ebony down. ⬤ 73

Jessie didn't know what to do, so she called the ⬤ 83
fire department. Soon fire fighters were on the scene ⬤ 92
with their tall ladders. After much work, they got ⬤ 101
Ebony out of the tree and into Jessie's arms. ⬤ 110

"Well, I guess I won't be entering you in the ⬤ 120
cat show," said Jessie. "But you sure put on a ⬤ 130
spectacular show for the neighbors." ⬤ 135

**Oral Reading Fluency Rubric**

| | Rubric Score | Comments: |
|---|---|---|
| **Phrasing and Fluency** | 1   2   3   4 | |
| **Intonation** | | |
| **Comprehension** | | |

**Rubric Score Key**
**1 and 2:** Student has not achieved an appropriate level of fluency for the level of the passage.
**3:** Fluent reading is being refined at the level of the passage.
**4:** Fluent reading has been achieved for the level at which the passage is written.

1. Jessie and Ebony are the main characters.
2. The cat ran up the tree so she could avoid getting a bath.
3. She called the fire department.
4. Getting Ebony out of the tree was the story's spectacular show.

Name_____ Date_____

Correct Words per Minute _____ National Norm of Words per Minute_____

# The Legislative Branch

The legislative branch of the United States government ____8
makes the laws for the country. The legislative branch ____17
has two parts: the Senate and the House of Representatives. ____27
Together, they are called Congress. Congress works in ____35
the Capitol Building in Washington, D.C. ____41

Every state elects people to serve in the Senate and ____51
the House of Representatives. These people are chosen ____59
to speak for the citizens in their states. ____67

The members of the Senate are called senators. ____75
Congress has one hundred senators. Each of the fifty ____84
states has two senators. The people elect senators to ____93
office for terms of six years. ____99

The members of the House of Representatives are ____107
called representatives. Congress has 435 representatives. ____112
The number of representatives a state has depends on ____122
the number of people who live in the state. The people ____132
elect representatives for terms of two years. ____139

Each representative comes from a district, or area, in ____148
his or her state. Representatives work on problems that ____157
are important to the people in their districts. ____165

**Oral Reading Fluency Rubric**

| | Rubric Score | Comments: |
|---|---|---|
| Phrasing and Fluency | 1  2  3  4 | |
| Intonation | 1  2  3  4 | |
| Comprehension | 1  2  3  4 | |

**Rubric Score Key**
**1 and 2:** Student has not achieved an appropriate
level of fluency for the level of the passage.
**3:** Fluent reading is being refined at the level
of the passage.
**4:** Fluent reading has been achieved for the
level at which the passage is written.

## Self-Check

1. Congress works in the Capitol Building in Washington, D.C.
2. Senators are in office for six years. Representatives are in office for two years.
3. They make laws for the country. People elect them to speak for the citizens in the states.

Name_____ Date_____

Correct Words per Minute _____ National Norm of Words per Minute _____

## The Rescue

6 "We'll have to wait for the
12 river to go down before we
15 cross," warned Mom.

19 "Look, the river's rising,
25 and the water is getting near
30 the cabin," Jordan alerted the
31 family.

36 As the water continued to
41 rise, Dad and Mom became
46 even more worried. They told
52 Jordan and me to pack up
57 and prepare to abandon the
62 cabin. Dad then called the
66 forest headquarters on his
68 cell phone.

73 "The ranger told me that
78 we should get to higher
83 ground because the river will
88 crest in about two hours,"
90 said Dad.

96 But it was too late. The
101 river had flowed over its
106 banks and there was no
110 escape route. We climbed
115 onto the cabin roof and
120 hoped the cabin would not
122 float away.

127 We survived the night on
132 the roof. The next morning
138 we were relieved to hear the
143 sound of a rescue helicopter
145 hovering overhead.

**Oral Reading Fluency Rubric**

| | Rubric Score | Comments: |
|---|---|---|
| Phrasing and Fluency | 1  2  3  4 | |
| Intonation | 1  2  3  4 | |
| Comprehension | 1  2  3  4 | |

**Rubric Score Key**
**1 and 2:** Student has not achieved an appropriate level of fluency for the level of the passage.
**3:** Fluent reading is being refined at the level of the passage.
**4:** Fluent reading has been achieved for the level at which the passage is written.

## Self-Check

1. The setting of the story is the family cabin by a river.
2. The escape route was flooded and they had nowhere else to go to escape the floodwaters.
3. A rescue helicopter hovering overhead made the family feel relief.
4. The ranger told Dad the river would crest.

Name_____ Date_____

Correct Words per Minute _____ National Norm of Words per Minute _____

# The Talking Dogfish

| 5 | Benson was a nosy guy |
| 10 | and was always looking for |
| 15 | interesting stories to write in |
| 18 | the school newspaper. |
| 22 | "What are you doing, |
| 25 | Martha?" asked Benson, |
| 29 | looking over his neighbor's |
| 30 | fence. |
| 35 | Martha was just sitting by |
| 38 | the garden pond. |
| 43 | "Go away, Benson. It's top |
| 49 | secret, and I don't want you |
| 54 | or anyone else to know |
| 58 | about it," said Martha. |
| 62 | "Oh, have you found |
| 65 | something interesting for |
| 71 | me to report in the school |
| 74 | newspaper?" inquired Benson. |

| 78 | Martha thought for a |
| 82 | minute, then smiled and |
| 88 | said, "Don't tell, but there's a |
| 92 | talking dogfish from Planet |
| 98 | Dingo in the pond. It was |
| 102 | delivered in this spaceship." |
| 106 | Just then Martha pulled |
| 111 | out a shiny silver machine |
| 116 | used to clean the garden |
| 117 | pond. |
| 121 | The following day, Benson's |
| 125 | newspaper report made the |
| 129 | front page: "Talking Dogfish |
| 134 | From Planet Dingo Lands in |
| 136 | Garden Pond!" |
| 140 | Benson had forgotten that |
| 146 | it was April Fools' Day, so |
| 152 | he didn't know the joke was |
| 154 | on him! |

**Oral Reading Fluency Rubric**

| | Rubric Score | | | |
|---|---|---|---|---|
| Phrasing and Fluency | 1 | 2 | 3 | 4 |
| Intonation | 1 | 2 | 3 | 4 |
| Comprehension | 1 | 2 | 3 | 4 |

**Comments:**

**Rubric Score Key**

**1 and 2:** Student has not achieved an appropriate level of fluency for the level of the passage.

**3:** Fluent reading is being refined at the level of the passage.

**4:** Fluent reading has been achieved for the level at which the passage is written.

## Self-Check

1. The main character is Benson.
2. He was a reporter for the school paper and always looking for an interesting story.
3. Martha told Benson there was a talking dogfish in her pond.
4. It was April Fools' Day.

Name_____ Date_____

Correct Words per Minute_____ National Norm of Words per Minute_____

## The Garage Sale

5 "OK, everybody, we have too
11 much stuff we never use. I'm
15 declaring this week family
20 clean-up week," said Ryan's dad.
26 "I want everyone to scour the
31 house and collect anything you
38 haven't used in the past year. On
44 Saturday we're going to have a
49 gigantic garage sale, and the
54 proceeds will be split evenly
57 among the family."

63 Ryan sorted through the stuff in
69 his room and found many things
76 that he didn't play with or wear
81 anymore. His sister found even
87 more stuff than Ryan did to
92 contribute to the garage sale.

97 Saturday soon came, and early
102 in the morning, people began
108 arriving like a swarm of locusts
112 descending on a cornfield.

120 "It looks as if our old junk is
124 everyone else's treasure," said
129 Ryan as people purchased their
130 stuff.

134 "Yes, selling your throwaways
140 has been my pleasure!" said Dad
148 as he gave Ryan his share of the
149 proceeds.

154 "And buying new treasure with
160 the proceeds will be my pleasure!"
163 said Ryan, smiling.

### Oral Reading Fluency Rubric

| | Rubric Score | | | | Comments: |
|---|---|---|---|---|---|
| Phrasing and Fluency | 1 | 2 | 3 | 4 | |
| Intonation | 1 | 2 | 3 | 4 | |
| Comprehension | 1 | 2 | 3 | 4 | |

### Rubric Score Key
**1 and 2:** Student has not achieved an appropriate level of fluency for the level of the passage.
**3:** Fluent reading is being refined at the level of the passage.
**4:** Fluent reading has been achieved for the level at which the passage is written.

## Self-Check

1. The problem is that the family had too much unused stuff in the house.
2. The family had a garage sale.
3. Proceeds were split evenly among family members.
4. He spent it on more stuff.

Name_____ Date _____

Correct Words per Minute_____ National Norm of Words per Minute _____

# The Pesky Flies

6     It was a particularly bad year
13 for flies, and they were always in
15 Justin's face.
22     "Let's buy some fly spray to get
28 rid of these pesky flies," suggested
29 Justin.
34     But his parents reminded him
41 that while fly spray might kill the
48 flies, it was also harmful to the
53 environment. So Justin began to
56 think about alternatives.
64     "I saw a man on TV wearing a
70 hat with corks dangling on strings
76 that kept flies away," said Justin.
81     "We'd look silly wearing hats
88 like that to work, school, and the
92 mall," protested Justin's mom.

98     "Hey, frogs eat pesky flies, and
105 we could raise frogs in our house,"
107 suggested Justin.
115     "I don't think it would be fair to
123 force frogs to live in tanks in our
127 house," objected Justin's dad.
131     Justin thought harder and
137 suddenly blurted out, "Oh, I know
143 something that'll get rid of the
151 flies. It's green like a frog and it
154 'eats' flies, too."
160     "A green spider or a green
164 vacuum cleaner?" responded his
165 mom.
170     "No, green Venus flytraps love
175 eating pesky flies!" said Justin.

## Oral Reading Fluency Rubric

| | Rubric Score | Comments: |
|---|---|---|
| Phrasing and Fluency | 1   2   3   4 | |
| Intonation | | |
| Comprehension | | |

**Rubric Score Key**
**1 and 2:** Student has not achieved an appropriate level of fluency for the level of the passage.
**3:** Fluent reading is being refined at the level of the passage.
**4:** Fluent reading has been achieved for the level at which the passage is written.

## Self-Check

1. The setting of the story is Justin's house.
2. The problem is that there were too many pesky flies.
3. It was harmful to the environment.
4. He suggested getting Venus flytraps, which would eat the flies.

Name _____ Date _____

Correct Words per Minute _____ National Norm of Words per Minute _____

# Land Sailing

5 Most weekends, Lara and her
12 family go land sailing on the dry
17 lakebed in a nearby desert.
21 "Remember your helmet and
26 gloves, Lara. You got enormous
32 blisters and rope burns on your
38 hands when you last went land
42 sailing without gloves," said
44 her dad.
49 Mom limped toward the car
53 holding a black-and-white checked
60 flag. She severely injured her leg in
66 a racing accident four years before,
73 so instead of racing, she now waves
80 the flag as the winners cross the
82 finish line.
89 "I'm going to see if I can
95 improve on my speed record from
103 last weekend by at least a few miles
107 per hour," said Lara's
109 brother, Reggie.
114 "I'm going to practice my
120 favorite trick—lifting one side of
126 my dirtboat off the ground while
132 zooming along on just two wheels,"
134 said Lara.
139 "You kids are speedsters and
144 tricksters, just like your mom,"
146 said Dad.
151 "You were the national dirtboat
158 champion for two years in a row,
166 Dad, so I think we take after you!"
168 said Reggie.
173 "Yes, but your mother taught
178 me everything I know about
182 dirtboats!" said Dad, laughing.

**Oral Reading Fluency Rubric**

| | Rubric Score | Comments: |
|---|---|---|
| **Phrasing and Fluency** | 1  2  3  4 | |
| **Intonation** | | |
| **Comprehension** | | |

**Rubric Score Key**
**1 and 2:** Student has not achieved an appropriate level of fluency for the level of the passage.
**3:** Fluent reading is being refined at the level of the passage.
**4:** Fluent reading has been achieved for the level at which the passage is written.

## Self-Check

1. The family enjoys land sailing, or dirtboating.
2. The activity takes place at a dried-up lakebed.
3. She now waves a black-and-white checked flag at the finish line rather than racing a dirtboat.
4. Lara and her brother like to go fast and do tricks.

# One-Minute Oral Reading Fluency Quick Check • Level V (see p. 267)

Name_____ Date_____

Correct Words per Minute _____ National Norm of Words per Minute_____

## Nebulas, Where Stars Are Born

9 — No matter what class a star is, all stars
18 — are born in the same way. They all begin
23 — in a nebula (NEH-byuh-luh). This is
32 — a thick cloud of gas and dust in space.
37 — Nebulas contain mainly hydrogen gas
44 — and a small amount of helium gas.
50 — There are different types of nebulas.
56 — Emission nebulas give off light. A
63 — reflection nebula reflects the light of stars
69 — around it. Planetary nebulas are formed
77 — when a sun-sized star dies and sheds its
84 — outer layers. A dark nebula is comprised
94 — of so much dust and gas that it blocks out
98 — all light around it.
104 — Dark nebula clouds are often very
110 — large, spanning across many millions of
116 — miles. And yet, astronomers believe that
122 — stars are born inside these nebulas.

129 — Inside the dark nebula, gas and dust
136 — stick together and form clumps. A large
143 — clump has more gravity. This gravity can
152 — pull other particles of gas and dust to the
158 — clump. With more particles, the clump
166 — increases in mass. Mass is the amount of
170 — matter that something contains.
176 — The gravity continues to pull the
182 — particles very close together. Sometimes a
189 — nearby star explodes and sends out shock
197 — waves. The shock waves can push the gas
203 — and dust particles even closer together.
208 — The thickly-packed gas and dust
216 — create a very hot, dense space in the
223 — center of the clump. Eventually this core
230 — will vaporize the dust. Then, the nebula
238 — collapses. The collapse of a nebula is the
243 — beginning of a star's birth.

### Oral Reading Fluency Rubric

| | Rubric Score | Comments: |
|---|---|---|
| Phrasing and Fluency | 1    2    3    4 | |
| Intonation | 1    2    3    4 | |
| Comprehension | 1    2    3    4 | |

### Rubric Score Key

**1 and 2:** Student has not achieved an appropriate level of fluency for the level of the passage.

**3:** Fluent reading is being refined at the level of the passage.

**4:** Fluent reading has been achieved for the level at which the passage is written.

## Self-Check

1. A nebula is a thick cloud of gas and dust in space.
2. The different types of nebulas are emissions nebulas, planetary nebulas, and dark nebulas.
3. A small clump pulls fewer particles because it has less gravity.
4. The important ideas in the passage are
   • all stars begin in nebulas,
   • gas and particles clump together inside nebulas,
   • the core of a nebula gets very dense and very hot,
   • a star is born when a nebula collapses.

Foundational Skills Assessments

Name_____ Date _____

Correct Words per Minute_____ National Norm of Words per Minute _____

## The Chernobyl Disaster

4      At 11 P.M. on April 25, 1986, nuclear
8      (NOO-klee-er) power plant workers in
11      Ukraine (yoo-KRANE) began running
17      a test on a reactor (ree-AK-ter). That's
23      the equipment that splits atoms without
32      causing an explosion. The test did not go as
33      planned.
37      About 1:23 A.M. on April 26, two
41      explosions rocked the Chernobyl-4
44      (cher-NOH-bul) reactor. Workers did
50      not realize how horrible the situation
58      was. People in nearby villages had no idea
65      that their lives had just been changed
66      forever.
72      During the testing at Chernobyl, the
77      splitting atoms overheated. The whole
85      process went too fast. Water in the reactor
91      turned into too much steam. Steam

99      pressure blew the lid off the reactor. The
104      shield that kept the radioactive (ray-dee-
110      oh-AK-tiv) materials in the reactor flew off.
116      Burning radioactive material burst out and
123      formed a cloud. Larger chunks of material
126      started several fires.
132      No one realized how much radioactive
139      material they were breathing in, or how
146      much was getting on their skin. Brave
154      people fought the fires. They saved the rest
160      of the plant from catching fire.
166      Many of the firefighters and workers
172      died or later had serious illnesses.
176      After the explosion, about 135,000
182      people had to leave their homes
188      permanently. The land and water were
195      terribly toxic. Villages as far as 20 miles (32
201      kilometers) away were no longer livable.

### Oral Reading Fluency Rubric

| | Rubric Score | | | | Comments: |
|---|---|---|---|---|---|
| Phrasing and Fluency | 1 | 2 | 3 | 4 | |
| Intonation | 1 | 2 | 3 | 4 | |
| Comprehension | 1 | 2 | 3 | 4 | |

**Rubric Score Key**
**1 and 2:** Student has not achieved an appropriate level of fluency for the level of the passage.
   **3:** Fluent reading is being refined at the level of the passage.
   **4:** Fluent reading has been achieved for the level at which the passage is written.

### Self-Check

1. A reactor is the equipment that splits atoms without causing an explosion.
2. Large chunks of burning radioactive material started fires.
3. People had to leave their homes because the land and water were toxic.
4. People can get sick when people come into contact with burning radioactive material.

# One-Minute Oral Reading Fluency Quick Check • Level X (see p. 271)

Name_____ Date_____

Correct Words per Minute _____ National Norm of Words per Minute _____

# Volcanoes: Nature's Awesome Power

(8) A volcano is any opening on Earth where
(15) material from inside the planet—molten rock,
(24) debris, and steam—makes its way to the surface.
(31) What causes a volcanic eruption? Volcanoes erupt
(39) when pressures within Earth force magma to the
(46) surface. Magma collects deep underground in a
(53) magma chamber. Under pressure, the magma rises
(62) and bursts through the crust in weak spots called
(69) vents. When pressure on the magma subsides,
(79) the eruption stops. This is much like a tube of
(86) toothpaste that you squeeze. The harder you
(94) squeeze, the more toothpaste squirts out. When you
(100) stop squeezing, you stop the flow.

(108) Three kinds of materials may erupt from a
(115) volcano: lava, tephra (rock fragments), and gases.
(125) Lava is magma that has reached the surface of a
(129) volcano. The terms pahoehoe (pah-HOH-ee-hoh-ee)
(136) and aa (AH-ah) are Hawaiian words that describe
(147) the lava flow. Aa is thick. Like honey or molasses, it
(156) flows slowly down the slopes. Pahoehoe is thin and

flows more quickly. When pahoehoe first erupts, (163)
get out of the way. This lava can outrun you! (173)

All volcanoes release gases during an eruption. (180)
The pressure of the gas in the magma causes the (190)
eruption. Some volcanoes erupt with more than (197)
just lava. If the magma contains a lot of gas, (207)
it will burst out violently with rock fragments (215)
called pyroclastic (PY-roh-KLAS-tik) materials. (218)
The pressure of the gas sends fragments of rock (227)
blasting out of the volcano. Some volcanoes (234)
alternate between eruptions of lava and eruptions of (242)
pyroclastic materials. (244)

Sometimes a tall column of pyroclastic materials (251)
and gases collapses. It races down the slope of the (261)
volcano at dangerous speeds in what is called a (270)
pyroclastic flow. The speed of these flows can reach (279)
120 miles per hour! (282)

When a volcano erupts, it can spew out (290)
anything from fine particles of dust to huge blocks (299)
of rock as big as a house. (306)

## Oral Reading Fluency Rubric

| | Rubric Score | | | | Comments: |
|---|---|---|---|---|---|
| Phrasing and Fluency | 1 | 2 | 3 | 4 | |
| Intonation | 1 | 2 | 3 | 4 | |
| Comprehension | 1 | 2 | 3 | 4 | |

### Rubric Score Key
**1 and 2:** Student has not achieved an appropriate level of fluency for the level of the passage.
**3:** Fluent reading is being refined at the level of the passage.
**4:** Fluent reading has been achieved for the level at which the passage is written.

## Self-Check

1. A volcano is any opening on Earth where material inside the planet makes its way to the surface.
2. Lava, tephra, and gases erupt from a volcano.
3. This passage is mostly about the force behind a volcanic eruption.
4. The temperature inside a volcano is very hot. It is hot enough to melt rock.

## Playing Ball

Tim and Jim play ball. They _____ 6
run. They jump. They throw _____ 11
the ball. They kick the ball. _____ 17
They have fun. _____ 20

"Time for bed!" says Mom. _____ 25

"Can we play more?" asks Tim. _____ 31

"You need to sleep now," _____ 36
says Mom. _____ 38

Tim and Jim go to bed. Mom _____ 45

tells them a story. The story _____ 51

is about two boys. The boys _____ 57

play ball. They run. They jump. _____ 63

They throw the ball. They kick _____ 69

the ball. The boys have fun. _____ 75

Tim and Jim smile. Soon the _____ 81

boys are asleep. _____ 84

**Self-Check**

1. Tim and Jim kicked the _____.
2. Why did Tim and Jim go to bed?
3. Did Tim and Jim like Mom's story? How can you tell?

## At the Park

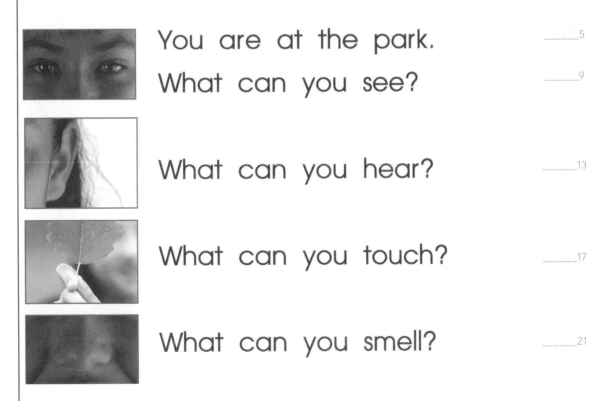

You are at the park. _____5

What can you see? _____9

What can you hear? _____13

What can you touch? _____17

What can you smell? _____21

 What can you taste? _____25

 You see grass. You see trees. _____31

 You hear kids. You hear dogs. _____37

 You slide on the slide. _____42

You swing on the swings. _____47

 You smell hot dogs. _____51

 Get a hot dog. Taste _____56

the hot dog. Mmm! _____60

## Water Fun

"Water, water, I love water!" ___5
said Lil. "I love to play in water." ___13

"I love to play in the sprinkler," ___20
said Tina. ___22

"I love to play in the pool," ___29
said Kim. ___31

"I love to play in the lake,"    ____38
said Shane.    ____40

"Water, water, I love water!"    ____45
said Lil. "I love to play    ____51
on water."    ____53

"How can you play *on* water?"    ____59
asked Shane.    ____61

"Water can freeze," said Lil.    ____66
"Then the water is ice.    ____71
I can skate on ice!"    ____76

## Here and There

I like to go to school. ___6

I can walk to school. ___11

I can ride my bike to school. ___18

I like to go to my friend's house. ___26

My mom takes me in a car. ___33

A car can take you far away. ___40

Sometimes I ride a bus to ____46
my friend's house. A bus ____51
can take you far away. ____56

I like to go to my grandma's ____63
house. We take a train to ____69

her house. A train can take ____75
you far, far away. ____79

Sometimes we take a plane ____84
to my grandma's house. A ____89
plane can take you far, far ____95
away. ____96

# The Moving Hat

Ann cannot find her cat.                            5
"Max!" Ann calls. "Where are                        10
you?" Max does not come.                            15

Ann looks for Max. Ann looks                        21
under her bed. Ann looks in                         27
the yard. She asks Mom and                          33
Dad, "Have you seen Max?"                           38

"No," say Mom and Dad.                              43

Ann goes to the living room.                        49
Her brother Mike is in the                          55
living room. Mike is looking at                     61
a hat. A hat is on the table.                       69

"What are you looking at?" Ann asks. _____ 74
_____ 76

"That hat keeps moving," says Mike. Ann looks at the hat. The hat *is* moving! Something is under the hat. Ann picks up the hat. _____ 80
_____ 85
_____ 91
_____ 95
_____ 101

"Max!" says Ann. "I have been looking for you." _____ 106
_____ 110

**Self-Check**

1. Ann could not find her _____.
2. Why was Mike looking at the hat?
3. How can you tell that Ann wanted to find Max?

## Juan Likes to Run

Juan likes to run. Juan runs    6
by himself. He runs with his    12
dog. He runs with his dad.    18
He runs with his friends.    23

When does Juan run? Juan    28
runs in the morning. He runs    34
in the afternoon. He runs in    40
the evening.    42

"I like to see you run, Juan,"    49
Mom says.    51

"I *like* to run," Juan says, _____57
running around Mom. _____60

"Do you know what time _____65
it is?" Mom asks. _____69

Juan looks at the clock. He _____75
takes small, slow steps. His _____80
mother smiles. Juan stops _____84
running. It is time for bed! _____90

**Self-Check**

1. **What does Juan like to do?**
2. **Why did Juan stop running?**
3. **What will Juan do when he gets up? How do you know?**

# The Walking Bus

Ten children at Park Lane School go                    7
home in the walking bus.                              12
Mrs. Green walks in front of                          18
the bus. Mr. Scott walks in back of                   26
the bus. The children walk in the                     33
middle.                                               34

"Here we go!" says Mrs. Green.                        40
"Look out for cars."                                  44

The bus walks slowly. It stops                        50
at Ben's house. It stops                              55
at Maria's house. It stops and stops                  62
until all ten children                                66
are home!                                             68

## Self-Check

1. What does a walking bus do?

2. Who walked in front of the walking bus?

3. How many children took the walking bus home?

4. Where did the walking bus stop?

# The Biggest Sunflower

Children at Sunset School were            5
growing sunflowers in the garden.         10
They watered their sunflowers to          15
help them grow. They talked to            21
their sunflowers to help them             26
grow.                                     27

But Maria put her sunflower in            33
a pot. All day long she moved the         41
pot to follow the sunshine.               46
Her sunflower grew very big.              51
It became the biggest sunflower.          56

"My sunflower likes sunshine," said       61
Maria. "So where the Sun goes, my         68
sunflower goes, too!"                     71

# Self-Check ✔️

1. What did the children grow in the school garden?

2. What did the children do to help their sunflowers grow?

3. Where did Maria put her sunflower?

4. How did Maria grow the biggest sunflower?

## Whose Shadow?

Kim, May, and Ben are playing. They _____7
are making shadows on the wall. They _____14
use their hands to make the shadows. _____21

"Look at my shadow!" says Kim. "Quack! _____28
My shadow is a duck." _____33

"Look at my shadow!" says May. "Meow! _____40
My shadow is a cat." _____45

"How about my shadow?" asks Ben. "Woof! _____52
My shadow is a little dog. Do you like _____61
my shadow?" _____63

"I like your shadow," says Kim. "But who _____ 71
is making the shadow of a *big* dog?" _____ 79

"Not me," says May. _____ 83

"Not me," says Ben. _____ 87

The children turn around. They see Ben's _____ 94
dog, Jake. Jake is making a shadow _____ 101
of his own. The children laugh. Jake is _____ 109
making the best shadow of all! _____ 115

**Self-Check**

1. **Kim, May, and Ben were making _____ on the wall.**
2. **How was Kim's shadow different from May's shadow?**
3. **How did Jake surprise the kids?**

# Bird Rescue

Mom and I were in the yard. I saw a        10
baby blue jay fly out of its nest. The        19
baby bird landed on the grass. Then        26
I saw Tabby, our cat! Tabby walked        33
slowly toward the bird.        37

"Mom! Tabby is going to get the baby        45
bird!" I cried.        48

Mom said, "Oh no! Save the bird!"        55

Then we saw a big blue jay fly over        64
Tabby's head. The big bird landed in        71
the grass. Tabby ran toward the big        78
bird. Tabby got very close. Then the        85
big blue jay flew away.        90

Tabby looked back at the baby bird. _____ 97
We looked, too. The baby bird flapped _____ 104
its tiny wings. Then the baby bird flew _____ 112
away! The big blue jay waited for the _____ 120
baby bird in the nest. _____ 125

The baby bird did not need our help _____ 133
after all. _____ 135

## Self-Check

1. A _____ flew out of its nest.

2. What happened after Tabby got close to the big blue jay?

3. How did the big blue jay help the baby blue jay?

# The Scruffy Dog

It was bath day for Mr. Green's dog. | 8
"Come here, Scruffy," said Mr. Green. | 14
"It's time for your bath." | 19

Scruffy didn't like to be washed with dog | 27
soap. He didn't like to be brushed with | 35
a dog comb. He liked to be scruffy and | 44
dirty. | 45

"Here I come, Scruffy," said Mr. Green. | 52
"You can't run away from me this time." | 60

Scruffy ran into the yard and hid | 67
from Mr. Green. But Mr. Green found | 74
him, and now Scruffy is fluffy! | 80

## Self-Check ✔

**1.** What day was it for Mr. Green's dog?

**2.** Why did Scruffy run away?

**3.** Where did Scruffy hide?

**4.** What did Mr. Green do when he found Scruffy?

# The Sleepy Dog

Sara had a cat, but she always wanted          8
to have a dog. "Jump, Snowy, jump," Sara        16
said to her cat. The cat just                   23
went to sleep. "Sit, Snowy, sit," Sara said to  32
her cat. The cat just went to sleep.            40

Then Sara went with her mom to look after       49
her grandpa's dog. "Run after                    54
the ball, Jack," Sara said to the dog.          62

He shut his eyes and went to sleep.             70

"Jack would make a very good cat!" said         77
Sara as she laughed.                            82

## Self-Check ✔

1. What kind of pet did Sara want?

2. Where did Sara go with her mom?

3. What did Sara's cat always do?

4. How was Grandpa's dog like Sara's cat?

## The Painting

Matt likes to paint. Matt paints pictures _____ 7
of things he sees outside. He paints _____ 14
pictures of cars. He paints pictures _____ 20
of trees. _____ 22

Meg is Matt's little sister. Meg watches _____ 29
Matt paint. "I want to paint, too," says _____ 37
Meg. "What can I paint?" _____ 42

Matt gets a big piece of paper. Matt _____ 50
puts the paper on the table. He gets _____ 58
some finger paints for Meg. He puts _____ 65
the finger paints on the table. _____ 71

"Now we can paint a picture together,"     _____ 78
says Matt.     _____ 80

First Meg paints. Meg uses her hands.     _____ 87
She makes green lines on the paper.     _____ 94
"I see grass outside," says Meg.     _____ 100

Then Matt paints. Matt uses a brush.     _____ 107
He paints a flower in the grass!     _____ 114

**Self-Check**

**1. Matt paints pictures of things he sees _____.**

**2. Why did Meg want to paint?**

**3. Matt was nice to his little sister. How can you tell?**

## Kim's Bad Day

Kim had a bad day. First, her brother _____ 8
ate the last bowl of Silly Shapes cereal. _____ 16
Kim had to eat her mother's boring _____ 23
wheat flakes. Then Kim missed the bus. _____ 30
She had to get a ride from her dad. _____ 39

Ms. Lopez gave the class a spelling test. _____ 47
Kim looked at the test and frowned. _____ 54
She had studied the wrong list of _____ 61
words! Ms. Lopez drew a sad face _____ 68
on Kim's test. Kim wanted to cry. _____ 75

Kim went home and showed her mother _____ 82
the spelling test. Mom made a sad face _____ 90
like the one Ms. Lopez drew on the test. _____ 99

Kim walked slowly to her room. Her eyes _____ 107
filled with tears. Then she bumped into _____ 114
something big and furry. She bumped _____ 120
into her dog, Buddy. Kim showed Buddy _____ 127
the test. Buddy did not frown. Buddy _____ 134
tried to eat the test! Kim laughed and _____ 142
hugged her dog, her Buddy. _____ 147

**Self-Check**

1. **Kim missed the _____.**

2. **Why did Kim frown when she looked at the spelling test?**

3. **Why is Buddy a good name for Kim's dog?**

# The Happy Robot

Robot sat down at the kitchen table. 7

"Would you like something to eat?" asked 14
Robot's owner. 16

"No, I'm not hungry," said Robot. But then it 25
ate 10 banana-nut muffins. "I 29
want to look at some of your wires," 37
said Robot's owner. She gently opened 43
the door to Robot's tummy and looked 50
inside. 51

"Your wires are messed up, so you eat 59
when you're not hungry." 63

When Robot was fixed, it smiled and said, 71
"Thank you for fixing me. Now I will not feel 81
so stuffed." 83

## Self-Check ✔

1. What did Robot eat?

2. If Robot was not hungry, why did it eat?

3. Who fixed Robot?

4. Why was Robot happy to be fixed?

# The Weather Watcher

The weather watcher watched the weather        6
every day. He told people watching TV        13
when it was going to be sunny, windy,        21
rainy, or snowy.        24

One day the weather watcher got tired        31
of watching the weather. He decided he        38
wanted to watch other things. So he went        45
on vacation.        48

He watched strong winds blow sailboats        54
over in the sea. He watched heavy rain        62
flood streets and sidewalks. Wherever he        68
went, the weather caused problems. So        74
he returned to watch the weather in        81
order to warn people when bad weather        88
was coming.        90

# Self-Check ✔

1. What did the weather watcher do?

2. Why did the weather watcher stop watching the weather?

3. What did the weather watcher see when he went on vacation?

4. Why did the weather watcher go back to watching the weather?

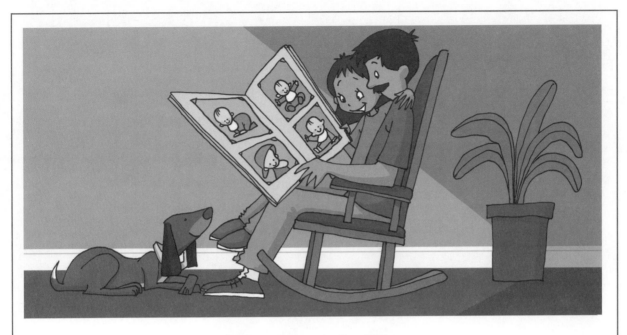

# All About Me

Lee's father was sitting in his favorite rocking _____8
chair. He was reading and smiling. "What are _____16
you reading?" Lee asked. _____20

"I'm reading a special book. The book is about _____29
a special person," said Lee's father. _____35

"Who is it?" Lee asked. Lee went up to the _____45
rocking chair and climbed onto her father's lap. _____53

Lee looked at the book. "The book has pictures _____62
of a baby," she said. "That baby is cute!" _____71

Lee's father said, "That baby is smart, too. That ____ 80
baby could say lots of words before age two. ____ 89
That baby even learned to walk all by herself." ____ 98

"Who is that cute, smart baby?" Lee asked. ____ 106

"It's you!" Lee's father said with a laugh. He ____ 115
hugged Lee. Lee hugged him back. ____ 121

## Self-Check

1. Lee's father was reading a special ____.

2. What did Lee do after she asked about the book?

3. How did Lee's father feel about the baby? How did Lee's father know the baby was smart?

# Princess Brat

Kate lived in a tiny house in the village. Kate _____10
was visiting Princess Brat's huge house for the _____18
first time. Kate brought a doll with her. "I want _____28
that doll," Princess Brat said. "Give her to me!" _____37

"No," Kate said calmly. "I will not give you my _____47
doll. But I will let you play with her." _____56

"You will let me play with your doll?" Princess _____65
Brat asked. _____67

"Sure," Kate said happily. _____71

Princess Brat was quiet. Then she said, "I will _____ 80
let you play with one of my dolls. Look inside _____ 90
my doll castle." _____ 93

"Wow! You have so many dolls!" Kate said. _____ 101
"I have only one doll." _____ 106

"Oh," said Princess Brat. She was quiet again. _____ 114
Then she said, "You can take some of my dolls _____ 124
home with you." _____ 127

Kate smiled and said, "You do not need a _____ 136
new doll, Princess Brat. But you *do* need _____ 144
a new name!" _____ 147

## Self-Check

1. Princess Brat lived in a huge _____.

2. How are Princess Brat and Kate different?

3. Why did Kate say, "But you *do* need a new name"?

# THE RED PIG

The baby pink pig looked at the other pigs. — 9

"You all need a bath," she said. "I'm not — 18
smelly, and I don't have mud all over me. — 27
I'm lovely, clean, and pink." — 32

The other pigs looked at the baby pig. Then — 41
they looked up at the hot sun and smiled. — 50
Soon the baby pig got hotter and hotter. She — 59
also got pinker and pinker. The pigs said, — 67
"You're lovely and clean, but you're not pink. — 75
Your skin is red." — 79

So the baby red pig jumped into the brown — 88
mud and was never, ever pink or red again! — 97

## Self-Check ☑

1. Who is the main character in the story?

2. What is the setting of the story?

3. What did the baby pig notice about the other pigs?

4. What did the baby pig do when her skin got red?

# MOLLY'S SMILE

Molly is 3 years old, and she doesn't talk very            9
much. When she was 2, her family waited and               17
waited for her to talk. But Molly just smiled and         27
didn't say much.                                          30

Molly's family took her to a children's doctor.           38
The doctor thought Molly just learned things              45
more slowly than other children. Molly didn't             52
talk to the doctor, but she gave him a big                62
smile.                                                    63

Her family took her to a speech teacher, who              72
helped Molly learn how to say words. Slowly,              80
Molly started to catch up with other children.            88

Molly still likes smiling. Her smile speaks               95
1,000 words!                                              96

# Self-Check

**1.** Who is the main character in the story?

**2.** What was the problem?

**3.** How was the problem solved?

**4.** What speaks 1,000 words?

# Mom's Birthday

    Today was Mom's birthday, so Tammy and I got up     10
early to bake a cake. Tammy read the recipe. I got     21
out the flour, sugar, cocoa, and cooking oil.     29

    "We also need two eggs, Sammy," said Tammy. I put     39
the eggs on the counter, but one egg rolled off.     49

    "Oops!" I picked up the broken egg shell. "I'll clean     59
the rest later," I said. Then we poured everything into     69
a big metal bowl. We set the electric mixer on high.     80

    "Oops!" I said again. Some of the cake batter flew     90
out of the bowl. "I think we should put the mixer on     102
*low*. We'll clean the walls later," I added.     110

We poured the rest of the batter into the pan and _____ 121
put the pan in the oven. We baked the cake before _____ 132
Mom woke up. She came into the kitchen just as we _____ 143
were frosting the cake. _____ 147

Boy, did Mom look surprised—and happy! _____ 154

## Self-Check

1. What did Sammy get out?

2. Why did some of the cake batter fly out of the bowl?

3. Why did Mom look surprised?

George Washington

Thomas Jefferson

Theodore Roosevelt

Abraham Lincoln

# The Meeting of the Mount Rushmore Presidents

"Good morning, Tom. Good morning, Teddy. Good morning, Abe," said George.

"Good morning to you, too," said Tom, Teddy, and Abe.

It was a beautiful morning at Mount Rushmore. Years ago, artists carved the faces of four presidents into the mountain. The sun lit up the faces of George Washington, Thomas Jefferson, Theodore Roosevelt, and Abraham Lincoln.

George said, "We need to vote on adding another president's face to our monument."

____7
____11

____19
____21

____29
____38
____48
____53
____57

____66
____71

"Four presidents are enough," said Tom. "George and I helped start the country. Abe kept it together during the Civil War. And Teddy did a fine job helping the country grow."

_____78
_____88
_____98
_____102

"We've discussed this already," said Abe. "We are presidents from the first 125 years of American history. We need to add a president from the past 100 years."

_____110
_____117
_____127
_____128

Teddy agreed. "I was the twenty-sixth president. More than a dozen new presidents have come and gone since then," he said.

_____135
_____144
_____149

"Surely one of them should have his face added to our monument," said George. "Whom would you suggest?"

_____159
_____166
_____168

## Self-Check

1. **When and where does this story take place?**

2. **What is the main conflict of the story?**

3. **Which president would you put on Mount Rushmore? Why?**

# The Rainbow Mailbox

Lana and her mom wanted to make a colorful mailbox. `9` `10`

"What kind of mailbox do you want to build?" asked Lana's mom. "How about a dinosaur mailbox?" `19` `27`

"That's not very colorful," replied Lana. "Why don't we build a rainbow mailbox of red, orange, yellow, green, blue, indigo, and violet?" `34` `43` `49`

"Then I think we'd better go to the paint store," said Lana's mom, laughing. `59` `63`

"Oops, we need eight colors. I forgot about gold paint for the pot of gold that's at the end of the rainbow!" said Lana. `72` `84` `87`

When the mail carrier saw the rainbow mailbox, she said to Lana, "Your mailbox makes me cheerful on rainy days!" `95` `104` `107`

## Self-Check ✔

1. Why didn't Lana want to build a dinosaur mailbox?

2. What did Lana and her mom almost forget at the paint store?

3. Why did they need the gold paint?

4. Why did the mail carrier like the rainbow mailbox?

# Scarecrow Joe

The old crows weren't afraid of Scarecrow Joe. — 8
Farmer Robin knew that she had to do something, — 17
so she dressed Joe in black clothes. — 24

"That will make you look scary," she said to — 33
Scarecrow Joe. — 35

But the crows thought that Joe looked like a big, — 45
black, friendly bird. They just kept eating Farmer — 53
Robin's corn. — 55

One day an eagle flew over the field and saw the — 66
crows eating Farmer Robin's corn. The eagle decided — 74
to help poor, frightened Scarecrow Joe by swooping — 82
down and scaring the crows. — 87

The eagle said, "I'm an eagle who scares crows," — 96
and sat on Joe's shoulder. From that day on, — 105
the eagle and the scarecrow kept Farmer Robin's — 113
corn safe. — 115

## Self-Check ✔

1. What is the setting of the story?

2. What did Farmer Robin do to make Scarecrow Joe look scary?

3. Why weren't the crows scared by Scarecrow Joe?

4. How did the problem get solved?

# The Cat Show

"I am going to enter Ebony in the big cat show, 11
but first I have to give her a bath," said Jessie. 22

Ebony sensed that she was about to get a bath and 33
scrambled up a tall cottonwood tree. Jessie pleaded 41
and pleaded for her to come down. But Ebony just 52
sat high up in the tree, ignoring Jessie's pleas. All the 62
neighbors came out and tried to help 69
Jessie get Ebony down. 73

Jessie didn't know what to do, so she called the 83
fire department. Soon fire fighters were on the scene 92
with their tall ladders. After much work, they got 101
Ebony out of the tree and into Jessie's arms. 110

"Well, I guess I won't be entering you in the 120
cat show," said Jessie. "But you sure put on a 130
spectacular show for the neighbors." 135

## Self-Check

1. Who are the main characters in the story?

2. Why did the cat run up the tree?

3. How did Jessie get the cat down from the tree?

4. What was the spectacular cat show in the story?

# The Legislative Branch

The legislative branch of the United States government    ___8
makes the laws for the country. The legislative branch    ___17
has two parts: the Senate and the House of Representatives.    ___27
Together, they are called Congress. Congress works in    ___35
the Capitol Building in Washington, D.C.    ___41

Every state elects people to serve in the Senate and    ___51
the House of Representatives. These people are chosen    ___59
to speak for the citizens in their states.    ___67

The members of the Senate are called senators.    ___75
Congress has one hundred senators. Each of the fifty    ___84
states has two senators. The people elect senators to    ___93
office for terms of six years.    ___99

The members of the House of Representatives are    _____107
called representatives. Congress has 435 representatives.    _____112
The number of representatives a state has depends on    _____121
the number of people who live in the state. The people    _____132
elect representatives for terms of two years.    _____139

Each representative comes from a district, or area, in    _____148
his or her state. Representatives work on problems that    _____157
are important to the people in their districts.    _____165

## Self-Check

1. Where does Congress work?

2. What is one way senators and representatives are different?

3. Why must senators and representatives be trustworthy?

# The Rescue

6_____      "We'll have to wait for the
12_____   river to go down before we
15_____   cross," warned Mom.

19_____      "Look, the river's rising,
25_____   and the water is getting near
30_____   the cabin," Jordan alerted the
31_____   family.

36_____      As the water continued to
41_____   rise, Dad and Mom became
46_____   even more worried. They told
52_____   Jordan and me to pack up
57_____   and prepare to abandon the
62_____   cabin. Dad then called the
66_____   forest headquarters on his
68_____   cell phone.

73_____      "The ranger told me that
78_____   we should get to higher

ground because the river will   _____83
crest in about two hours,"   _____88
said Dad.   _____90

     But it was too late. The   _____96
river had flowed over its   _____101
banks and there was no   _____106
escape route. We climbed   _____110
onto the cabin roof and   _____115
hoped the cabin would not   _____120
float away.   _____122

     We survived the night   _____126
on the roof. The next morning   _____132
we were relieved to hear the   _____138
sound of a rescue helicopter   _____143
hovering overhead.   _____145

## Self-Check ✔

1. What is the setting of the story?

2. Why did the family climb onto the roof?

3. What caused them to be relieved the next morning?

4. How did Dad know the river would crest?

# The Talking Dogfish

5 Benson was a nosy guy
10 and was always looking for
15 interesting stories to write in
18 the school newspaper.

22 "What are you doing,
25 Martha?" asked Benson,
29 looking over his neighbor's
30 fence.

35 Martha was just sitting by
38 the garden pond.

43 "Go away, Benson. It's top
49 secret, and I don't want you
54 or anyone else to know
58 about it," said Martha.

62 "Oh, have you found
65 something interesting for
71 me to report in the school
74 newspaper?" inquired Benson.

78 Martha thought for a
82 minute, then smiled and
88 said, "Don't tell, but there's a
92 talking dogfish from Planet
98 Dingo in the pond. It was
102 delivered in this spaceship."

106 Just then Martha pulled
111 out a shiny silver machine
116 used to clean the garden
117 pond.

121 The following day, Benson's
125 newspaper report made the
129 front page: "Talking Dogfish
134 From Planet Dingo Lands in
136 Garden Pond!"

140 Benson had forgotten that
146 it was April Fools' Day, so
152 he didn't know the joke was
154 on him!

## Self-Check ✔

1. Who is the main character in the story?

2. Why was Benson so nosy?

3. What did Martha tell Benson was in her pond?

4. Why was Martha playing a joke on Benson?

# The Garage Sale

5    "OK, everybody, we have too
11    much stuff we never use. I'm
15    declaring this week family
20    clean-up week," said Ryan's dad.
26    "I want everyone to scour the
31    house and collect anything you
38    haven't used in the past year. On
44    Saturday we're going to have a
49    gigantic garage sale, and the
54    proceeds will be split evenly
57    among the family."

63    Ryan sorted through the stuff in
69    his room and found many things
76    that he didn't play with or wear
81    anymore. His sister found even
87    more stuff than Ryan did to
92    contribute to the garage sale.

97    Saturday soon came, and early
102    in the morning, people began
108    arriving like a swarm of locusts
112    descending on a cornfield.

120    "It looks as if our old junk is
124    everyone else's treasure," said
129    Ryan as people purchased their
130    stuff.

134    "Yes, selling your throwaways
140    has been my pleasure!" said Dad
148    as he gave Ryan his share of the
149    proceeds.

154    "And buying new treasure with
160    the proceeds will be my pleasure!"
163    said Ryan, smiling.

## Self-Check

**1.** What is the problem presented in the story?

**2.** How was the problem resolved?

**3.** How did the family split the proceeds from the garage sale?

**4.** What did Ryan do with his share of the proceeds?

# The Pesky Flies

6     It was a particularly bad year
13 for flies, and they were always in
15 Justin's face.

22     "Let's buy some fly spray to get
28 rid of these pesky flies," suggested
29 Justin.

34     But his parents reminded him
41 that while fly spray might kill the
48 flies, it was also harmful to the
53 environment. So Justin began to
56 think about alternatives.

64     "I saw a man on TV wearing a
70 hat with corks dangling on strings
76 that kept flies away," said Justin.

81     "We'd look silly wearing hats
88 like that to work, school, and the
92 mall," protested Justin's mom.

    "Hey, frogs eat pesky flies, and 98
we could raise frogs in our house," 105
suggested Justin. 107

    "I don't think it would be fair to 115
force frogs to live in tanks in our 123
house," objected Justin's dad. 127

    Justin thought harder and 131
suddenly blurted out, "Oh, I know 137
something that'll get rid of the 143
flies. It's green like a frog and it 151
'eats' flies, too." 154

    "A green spider or a green 160
vacuum cleaner?" responded his 164
mom. 165

    "No, green Venus flytraps love 170
eating pesky flies!" said Justin. 175

## Self-Check ✔

1. What is the setting of the story?

2. What is the problem?

3. What was wrong with using fly spray to get rid of the flies?

4. How did Justin resolve the problem?

# Land Sailing

5 Most weekends, Lara and her
12 family go land sailing on the dry
17 lakebed in a nearby desert.
21 "Remember your helmet and
26 gloves, Lara. You got enormous
32 blisters and rope burns on your
38 hands when you last went land
42 sailing without gloves," said
44 her dad.
49 Mom limped toward the car
53 holding a black-and-white checked
60 flag. She severely injured her leg in
66 a racing accident four years before,
73 so instead of racing, she now waves
80 the flag as the winners cross the
82 finish line.
89 "I'm going to see if I can
95 improve on my speed record from

103 last weekend by at least a few miles
107 per hour," said Lara's
109 brother, Reggie.
114 "I'm going to practice my
120 favorite trick—lifting one side of
126 my dirtboat off the ground while
132 zooming along on just two wheels,"
134 said Lara.
139 "You kids are speedsters and
144 tricksters, just like your mom,"
146 said Dad.
151 "You were the national dirtboat
158 champion for two years in a row,
166 Dad, so I think we take after you!"
168 said Reggie.
173 "Yes, but your mother taught
178 me everything I know about
182 dirtboats!" said Dad, laughing.

## Self-Check ✔

1. What activity does the family in the story enjoy?

2. Where does the activity take place?

3. How has Lara's mom's involvement in the activity changed since her accident?

4. Why does Lara's dad call her and her brother tricksters and speedsters?

# Nebulas, Where Stars Are Born

No matter what class a star is, all stars are born in the same way. They all begin in a nebula (NEH-byuh-luh). This is a thick cloud of gas and dust in space. Nebulas contain mainly hydrogen gas and a small amount of helium gas.

There are different types of nebulas. Emission nebulas give off light. A reflection nebula reflects the light of stars around it. Planetary nebulas are formed when a sun-sized star dies and sheds its outer layers. A dark nebula is comprised of so much dust and gas that it blocks out all light around it.

Dark nebula clouds are often very large, spanning across many millions of miles. And yet, astronomers believe that stars are born inside these nebulas.

Inside the dark nebula, gas and dust stick together and form clumps. A large clump has more gravity. This gravity can pull other particles of gas and dust to the clump. With more particles, the clump increases in mass. Mass is the amount of matter that something contains.

The gravity continues to pull the particles very close together. Sometimes a nearby star explodes and sends out shock waves. The shock waves can push the gas and dust particles even closer together.

The thickly-packed gas and dust create a very hot, dense space in the center of the clump. Eventually this core will vaporize the dust. Then, the nebula collapses. The collapse of a nebula is the beginning of a star's birth.

9
18
23
32
37
44
50
56
63
69
77
84
94
98
104
110
116
122
129
136
143
152
158
166
170
176
182
189
197
203
208
216
223
230
238
243

## Self-Check ✔

1. What is a nebula?

2. What are the different types of nebulas?

3. Does a small clump pull more or fewer particles than a large clump? How do you know?

4. What are the important ideas in this passage?

# The Chernobyl Disaster

4     At 11 P.M. on April 25, 1986, nuclear
8     (NOO-klee-er) power plant workers in
11     Ukraine (yoo-KRANE) began running
17     a test on a reactor (ree-AK-ter). That's
23     the equipment that splits atoms without
32     causing an explosion. The test did not go as
33     planned.

37     About 1:23 A.M. on April 26, two
41     explosions rocked the Chernobyl-4
44     (cher-NOH-bul) reactor. Workers did
50     not realize how horrible the situation
58     was. People in nearby villages had no idea
65     that their lives had just been changed
66     forever.

72     During the testing at Chernobyl, the
77     splitting atoms overheated. The whole
85     process went too fast. Water in the reactor
91     turned into too much steam. Steam

99     pressure blew the lid off the reactor. The
104     shield that kept the radioactive (ray-dee-
110     oh-AK-tiv) materials in the reactor flew off.
116     Burning radioactive material burst out and
123     formed a cloud. Larger chunks of material
126     started several fires.

132     No one realized how much radioactive
139     material they were breathing in, or how
146     much was getting on their skin. Brave
154     people fought the fires. They saved the rest
160     of the plant from catching fire.

166     Many of the firefighters and workers
172     died or later had serious illnesses.

176     After the explosion, about 135,000
182     people had to leave their homes
188     permanently. The land and water were
195     terribly toxic. Villages as far as 20 miles (32
201     kilometers) away were no longer livable.

# Self-Check

**1.** What is a reactor?

**2.** What started fires?

**3.** How did the events of April 26, 1986 affect the people living near the nuclear power plant?

**4.** What happens to people when they come into contact with radioactive material?

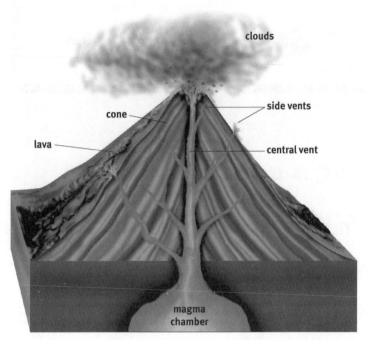

clouds

cone

side vents

lava

central vent

magma chamber

diagram of a volcanic eruption

# Volcanoes: Nature's Awesome Power

8     A volcano is any opening on Earth where
15 material from inside the planet—molten rock,
24 debris, and steam—makes its way to the surface.
31 What causes a volcanic eruption? Volcanoes erupt
39 when pressures within Earth force magma to the
46 surface. Magma collects deep underground in a
53 magma chamber. Under pressure, the magma rises
62 and bursts through the crust in weak spots called
69 vents. When pressure on the magma subsides,
79 the eruption stops. This is much like a tube of
86 toothpaste that you squeeze. The harder you
94 squeeze, the more toothpaste squirts out. When you
100 stop squeezing, you stop the flow.
108     Three kinds of materials may erupt from a
115 volcano: lava, tephra (rock fragments), and gases.
125 . Lava is magma that has reached the surface of a
129 volcano. The terms pahoehoe (pah-HOH-ee-hoh-ee)
136 and aa (AH-ah) are Hawaiian words that describe
147 the lava flow. Aa is thick. Like honey or molasses, it
156 flows slowly down the slopes. Pahoehoe is thin and

163 flows more quickly. When pahoehoe first erupts,
173 get out of the way. This lava can outrun you!
180     All volcanoes release gases during an eruption.
190 The pressure of the gas in the magma causes the
197 eruption. Some volcanoes erupt with more than
207 just lava. If the magma contains a lot of gas,
215 it will burst out violently with rock fragments
218 called pyroclastic (PY-roh-KLAS-tik) materials.
227 The pressure of the gas sends fragments of rock
234 blasting out of the volcano. Some volcanoes
242 alternate between eruptions of lava and eruptions of
244 pyroclastic materials.
251     Sometimes a tall column of pyroclastic materials
261 and gases collapses. It races down the slope of the
270 volcano at dangerous speeds in what is called a
279 pyroclastic flow. The speed of these flows can reach
282 120 miles per hour!
290     When a volcano erupts, it can spew out
299 anything from fine particles of dust to huge blocks
306 of rock as big as a house.

## Self-Check ✔

1. What is a volcano?

2. What types of materials erupt from a volcano?

3. What is this passage mainly about?

4. Describe the temperature inside a volcano.